"Soul"utions

Lynne,

Let the world take you.
Allow it to nurture you.
Make it your world.

Michelle Paxton

"Soul"utions

Achieving Financial, Intellectual, Physical, Social, and Spiritual Balance with Soul

M. A. Payton

Award-winning Author of
Adventures of a Mainstream Metaphysical Mom

The Left Side
Powell, Ohio

Interior body text is set in 12 point Centar by Pete Masterson, Æonix
Publishing Group, www.aeonix.com
Cover illustration by Prescott Hill, copyright by Michelle Payton
Interior illustrations copyright by Michelle Payton

ISBN 0-9719804-1-1
LCCN: 2004090236

Published by
The Left Side
437 Hopewell Drive
Powell, Ohio 43065

Phone: 614-785-9821
Fax: 614-785-9819
www.theleftside.com

Printed in the United States of America

Contents

Contents

Social 137

"Let us live while we live."

—Phillip Doddridge, Quoted in
"Job Orton's Life of Doddridge" (1764)

Spiritual 155

". . Spirit is an invisible force made visible in all life."

—Maya Angelou, "In the Spirit," Wouldn't
Take Nothing for my Journey Now (1993)

Processing 185

> *"Many of the insights of the saint stem from his experience as a sinner."*
>
> —*Eric Hoffer, "The Passionate State of Mind" (1954)*

Introduction

"The soul is the voice of the body's interests."
—*George Santayana, The Life of Reason:*
Reason in Art (1905-06)

I WONDERED... AFTER RECEIVING so many supportive comments on *Adventures of a Mainstream Metaphysical Mom*, if this book would be as helpful, informative, life altering (as some readers reported) and as practical a guide to living or is it just the "next book?" Is this an attempt to come out with the next big idea because my first published piece gave me the confidence to complete the next? The answer... As I continue to pour my heart onto paper, I'm certain that I am divinely guided. Certainly, I take full responsibility for the ideas on the pages that I have written. However, I am certain that there are words or phrases planted in each book, published under my name, just for you. When you discover the ten words in this book that create a positive outcome for you then we both have been truly blessed.

As I continue to listen to my inner voice and recognize the everyday miracles and messages revealed, stories emerge. But all roads seem to be pointing in the same direction, everything seems to come full circle back to balance which includes connecting with your soul. With this comes a great deal of frustration, however, because everyday life can be a real pain. On one hand, we work (defined differently by everyone) to live. On the other hand, many times, it feels like we are fooling ourselves as most of our waking hours seem to be focused on a grueling circle of tasks.

Basically our lives are split into thirds, one third is sleeping, another third is working (domestic, professional, non-profit...) and the balance is spent on everything else. Coinciding with our work, sleep, and play patterns are our areas of life. These include your financial, intellectual, physical, social and spiritual realities. I use these five categories as a soul map and life coach myself and others to achieve balance. A soul map is an actionable plan that combines non-physical (soul level) and physical goals. We have the capability of creating a reality that is perfect to our relative standards in every area of life. The key is being conscious when making choices by following our intuition, being aware that everything happens for a reason, and having gratitude for what we have, acknowledging that we are all pieces to one big puzzle empowered with choices to reach an outcome. It doesn't matter what business or life focus is chosen, these ideas point us in the direction of perfection as we see it from our own eyes. While we can't control our lives, we can help guide them by feeling our way to a soul-balanced happiness. We can make time for ourselves. We can wrap our arms around life, and have a sense of completion.

This doesn't mean that we have all the answers. However it could mean that we could discover what we were born to do for that moment. I say "the moment" because life takes its zigs and zags and adds spice to our lives. After all, if we're not learning (sometimes by the seat of our pants) what's the point? It would be like reading the last chapter of a book before you read the first 200 pages, watching the end of a movie before you sit through the other hour and fifty minutes. We get our thrills by working our way toward "the" answers.

But sometimes the glass is half empty or simply has no water in it at all. How do we follow our intuition when the world says "just the facts!" How do we embrace the idea that everything happens for a reason when a project sours, or worse, we lose our jobs? How do we have gratitude for what we have when we always feel like we don't have enough? How can we believe that we are all one when we are physically or mentally attacked by other "ones?" There is more pressure to produce as a parent, significant other and/or professional than ever. Maintaining boundaries between work and family is increasingly difficult. There is a lot of unhappiness in our world for a lot of reasons but we each are in charge of achieving "Soul"utions.

Let's take a journey together to look at our, and others', core interests, ideas, values, and visions. We'll see how others achieve or don't achieve their goals, holding the vision that this will assist us in achieving "the good life" that falls under the categories of Financial, Intellectual, Physical, Social and Spiritual. Last, but not least, you will learn how to soul map. We'll determine your life path and set personal and professional short and long-term goals to achieve soul fulfillment.

Financial

"... Know thine opportunity."

— Pittacua (7th-6th C. B.C.), Quoted in Diogenes Laertius
"Lives and Opinions of Eminent Philosophies" (3rd C.A.D.)

What Really Excites You When You "Work"?

*"Anyone who has achieved excellence in any form knows that it comes
as a result of ceaseless concentration."*

—Louise Brooks, "The Other Face of W.C. Fields,
Lulu in Hollywood" (1982)

I CHOSE NOT TO LEAVE MY FAMILY for entire weekends many times
when promoting my personal work. To accomplish my goal
I would, generally, drive three to five hours straight through
(sometimes eight). Many times I would make these drives all in one
day to get back home the same day. But day trips didn't bring in a
whole lot of cash. Driving nearly seven hours in one day, I brought

home one hundred dollars, another weekend one hundred forty-five, still another two hundredish and when I had to pay for an overnight stay I ate really light.

My day job, my international wholesale business, was paying my bills so my personal work was extra pocket money. That felt good but in the back of my mind I would wonder, Am I really accomplishing anything? Am I making a difference? It seemed almost too simple to me. When I put things to paper when working with people individually, I regularly wondered if I was really helping them improve their lives. Then I received a sign.

I was in a board meeting with a number of my peers (we were mostly volunteers) and one of the board members said, "I am resigning my post, to increase my quality of life… I'm taking more time off… I'm taking care of myself… I'm even gardening!… And it started with my coaching session with Michelle." A big smile swept over my face. While I was sorry to see him leave our monthly conference call and bonding ceremony, I was thrilled that my individual Soul Mapping work was making a difference in his life.

So when you ask yourself, "What excites me when I work?" ask these simple questions:

- How have I helped others move forward in the past?
- How am I currently helping others to move forward?
- How can I help others move forward in the future?

You don't have to be a medical doctor to save lives. Do you say "good morning" to those in need of a friendly word? Do you thank those who are helping you daily? Do you come to the aid of others in need daily? Make your past, present and future list to understand the light being that you have been, are and can be in the future. How do you celebrate your accomplishments?

What Really Matters

"Accidents will happen even in the best regulated families."
—Charles Dickens, "David Copperfield" (1849-50)

IT WAS A BEAUTIFUL DAY, about 75 degrees and sunny. Instead of driving to the post office and bank, I decided to ride my bike and take my two-year-old as well. We'd completed our errands, my daughter was enjoying the sucker that she got from the bank teller and as we were on the crosswalk a car turned left into our bicycle.

Every mother would like to think that she is selfless enough to lay down her life for her children and I was amazed at what transpired in those few moments. Surreal, we were in the middle of the crosswalk and the car hit the middle of my bicycle (with my child and me on it). I jumped onto the car hood, continuing to hold the bike handles so that my baby didn't fall or get caught near the tires of the car, then I jumped on the road (flat on my feet). The bike's front tire was in the air, and my baby's body never once touched the ground. We both had on our helmets and she was safely strapped into her seat. I had a few scratches on the leg between the bike and the car, but otherwise we were both fine, so fine, in fact, that my toddler still had her sucker in one hand and her "no spill" milk cup in the other.

A witness said that I screamed so loud that the whole town could have heard it. (I have no recollection of this.) My next thought was to keep my daughter from being afraid of riding on the bicycle or thinking anything was wrong, so I got to the other side of the road. Police were there in minutes. I checked my baby but was advised not to take her out of her seat until the ambulance checked her out. She was fine with this because a lot of people were gathered around and she decided to be a little shy in her seat and continue to work on her sucker. I released a little (some tears and some shaking), but limited it so as not to upset my little one. The driver, a young man in his twenties, was saying, "I know it's all my fault." I felt warmth and compassion for this frightened young man and responded, "Yes, it was, but you had no intention of this happening. We're okay so not to worry. You didn't wake up this morning with the goal of ramming your vehicle into a mother and her baby." He went on to say that he needed to slow down, and pay closer attention to his driving. I agreed, but assured him that we were fine. Upon leaving he hugged me and said, "I am so sorry." I responded, "I know you are."

Once my baby was checked out, I said, "Well if that isn't angelic intervention, I don't know what is!" The emergency technicians said, "Yeah, those sorts of things can happen." The police asked me if I needed a ride home but I just wanted to ride this off, make sure that the baby knew the bike was safe and reconnect with the elements that we began our trip with.

I parked the bike. My toddler went on her way to her next project and I just had to shake my head in amazement and gratitude. I don't fear death but I would like to stay around for as long as possible in this physical life to be a part of my children's lives. I feel like I can protect and teach them like nobody else can. Were we just an instrument for this driver's lesson(s)? Are there accidents? In my mind, accidents are lessons and lessons happen for a reason. So I'm celebrating what's most important as I appreciate my synchronistic life. What really matters? What are my true top priorities? Is it my job that keeps me sustained, my car, my home, my clothes or the fact that I have people I love and who love me back no matter what my appearance or titles?

Intuitive versus Modern Science

"Preserving the health by too severe a rule is a wearisome malady."
—*La Rochefoucauld, "Maxims" (1665)*

THE NIGHT OF THE BIKE ACCIDENT, I had an appointment to keep with some people, many of whom were professional psychics and healers. I was feeling fine and felt like I should just move on. I was fine until I got out of my vehicle. All of a sudden (about six hours after the accident), my left foot began to cramp and spasm. Thinking it was just a little cramp, I decided to walk it off but it got progressively worse. One psychic/healer put his hand over my foot and said, "It feels like a hair line fracture." Very uncomfortable, I made it back to my vehicle and said that I would have to do this another time and I was going to the local emergency room.

By the time I got there I was in excruciating pain. My husband carried me into the lobby and they proceeded to check me out. The doctor said that he couldn't figure out what was wrong and that my x-rays showed no problems. Oddly, we went home with lots of drugs and I got a good night's rest but he didn't recommend how I should take care of my foot, didn't send me home with crutches (aware that I couldn't walk on it), or tell me when I should apply pressure (walk on it).

Next day, the foot felt better but I still couldn't walk on it. When I called another friend that was at the meeting to give her an explanation as to why I had to leave so quickly, she said, "I sensed a hair line fracture in your foot." This was the second time I heard this from an intuitive person I trust. But the doctor didn't find this and there was no way of convincing him to take another look at the foot. In fact, he said, "I don't know what's wrong." So I called a friend who is an emergency room doctor and said,

"Let's assume that I have a hair line fracture in my foot. What would you prescribe?" To play it safe, I assumed I had a hair line fracture to get the best healing results, and my husband resized some old crutches of his so I wouldn't apply too much pressure on my foot.

It was important to get to medical facilities, but a good doctor will be the first to tell you that he/she is not God. And this doctor simply said, "I don't know what's wrong." It can be frustrating when there isn't a label for your pain. But this time, it was time to celebrate that fact that I had access to people that could apply modern day technology to heal and those who could intuitively heal. Combined, they make an awesome healing team. Have you done research on reliable sources of alternative healing? Explored when it is best to use alternative and mainstream techniques and when to combine them as well?

Being Held Back... Are We Really?

"What a curious creature is man! With what a variety of powers and faculties is he endued! Yet how easily is he disturbed and put out of order!"

—*James Boswell, London Journal, March 22, 1763*

THE MOST FRUSTRATING PART about being physically or mentally held back (or, at least, perceived) is watching things pass you by that you'd like to be a part of whether that means leisure activity or new business opportunities.

The weather had been beautiful but I was a bit cranky because my foot injury from the bike/car accident didn't allow me to do what I would like to do... ride my bike, take a walk, and sleep comfortably. I wasn't mortally wounded but it seemed that this was just the beginning of my many escapades for the next couple of weeks.

By the end of this week, the Internal Revenue Service informed me that I was on their audit list and we were to meet in ten days (they mailed my notification to the wrong address and I should have received this information two weeks prior). Then my computer went on the fritz and I was on the phone with several computer technicians for four hours. The following week wasn't showing any improvement as new challenges reared their ugly heads.

As the "attacks" continued, I noticed that I couldn't make a huge deal out of most of these incidents. I found myself sinking into a space of low focus. I was numb and could only respond, "What next... Whatever... Bring it on..." (pretty much in that order). In fact, as I typed this section—it sounds silly, but—I even had a nagging paper cut on the tip of my finger and it was making it uncomfortable for me to type.

What did it all mean? I'm guessing I just needed to be low key. Ride my bicycle very slowly. Go to bed earlier. Eat less fatty, more healthy foods with my body not being able to move as quickly and integrate this back into my life. Maybe consider yoga, so I made the call to attend a beginner's class. Was I being held back from the things that I thought I should've been doing but the Universe was saying "not yet?" What opportunities were opening to me as I slowed down? What should I be letting go of to move onto the next level? What changes was I looking to make in my life? I really got into a "cut the crap" mode. In the stillness comes the light of knowing that it's time for changes—but silence can be really uncomfortable. How do you feel with not completely knowing what changes are around the corner? How do you bring yourself to a place of peace knowing that the only constant is change?

Are You Ever Really Without? Exercising your gratitude muscles.

"The honest poor man can sometimes forget poverty. The honest rich man can never forget it." —G.K. Chesterton, *"Cockneys and Their Jokes, All Things Considered"* (1908)

THROUGHOUT MY CHILDHOOD, I was never aware of a time that we didn't have enough to eat. As I understand it now, my mother mentioned that there was a period of time where she had a difficult time keeping food on the table (during the more intense drinking periods of my father). My perception is that she made a personal creed after that tough period because, for as long as I could remember, she would feed half the neighborhood baking cookies and over-preparing meals. Maybe I assimilated my mom's goal, because my cupboards are packed full of food to this day.

The Universe provides ample opportunity for us to experience, and make adjustments. For my mom it was when she couldn't feed her children. For me it was when I was about 12 years old and I had a boyfriend that had, what we called in my day (can't believe I just said that), fever blisters. We didn't know what herpes simplex was nor did we have any idea that it was incredibly contagious and a condition, once contracted, to be managed for a lifetime.

I ended up getting a really bad case of "fever blisters" on and in my mouth. I didn't know, nor did my mother, how to treat them effectively. Petroleum jelly was to first aid in my household like duct tape was to universal fix-it guys. And since these little lesions looked like cuts and felt like burns, I figured petroleum jelly would do the trick. What I unknowingly did was create a protective coating on the virus (really gross, I know) and it spread all over the inside and outside of my mouth.

After several days of pain and the inability to eat without the inside of my mouth feeling like it was on fire, my mom took me to the pediatrician and he had to pull the coats of infection off so the blisters were exposed to air and would clear. Taking much more time to heal, I was completely unable to eat and found myself crying in front of the television as food commercials aired because I was, literally, starving. What excruciating physical pain it was to not eat! How thankful was I to know that not having food was a temporary condition! Life lessons occur in mysterious ways.

A friend of mine from high school had two beautiful children and her husband was in the military. He was stationed overseas (non-active duty) and she stayed behind in the States. Within a short time period she stopped receiving checks from her husband. She didn't have a job, couldn't afford a babysitter so she could work, and her income was measured from the previous year and her legal marital status (and the fact that she was supposed to be receiving support). For some time she couldn't get any kind of temporary assistance to get on her feet.

I didn't know this was going on until one day I suggested I come over and bring a bucket of chicken over for a fun meal. I noticed that my friend had lost a lot of weight and when I mentioned it to her she said that she started an exercise program to slim down a bit. Not thinking much about it, I went into her refrigerator to get something to drink and noticed that the refrigerator was completely bare with exception of milk for the baby. She was starving and I was in college with very few options myself. She, inevitably, got a divorce and got on her feet, but she was in the ultimate survival mode. "How do I feed two small children and keep up my strength at the same time?"

There are many small instances that develop your empathy muscles hence giving you a sense of gratitude. Do you have the basics like food, shelter and clothing? If you're missing any of those, what do you have? My father was a twisted and confused individual in this lifetime but I remember him coming down to our kitchen barefoot in the winter and doing a little dance celebration because our floor was warm (a major improvement from our previous, now condemned and torn down, rental home). My mother reminisces about how much we (my siblings and I) loved the warm Jiffy™ Gingerbread that she would whip together (33¢ a box) for us with a dab of whipped cream. Or the excitement in my mother's voice when she called my girlfriend's house (when I was in high school) to tell me that we had carpet on our steps (replacing the old broken linoleum). Equally excited, I told my girlfriend and her family the great news but they (living in a well-kept and carpeted home) weren't as impressed.

Remember that if you have food in your refrigerator, clothes on your back, and a roof over your head, you're richer than 75% of the world. Celebrate your fortune! Appreciate your intellectual opportunities as most don't even know how to read! Adore your physical body! Value your social and spiritual relationships as billions of people can't even go to a spiritual-driven gathering without the fear of harassment, arrest, torture or death.

How are you exercising your gratitude muscles so that you can truly celebrate your life?

Loving Who We Are When We "Work"

"Work is not the curse, but drudgery is."
—*Henry Ward Beecher, Proverbs*
from Plymouth Pulpit (1887)

I'VE "WORKED" FOR AS LONG AS I can remember. Elementary school age I made potholders and sold them door-to-door. Early teens I babysat and did cleaning jobs (houses, yards, cars, etc.). By sixteen I worked in a number of restaurants doing various jobs eventually landing a nice paying job in college as a relief supervisor in nutrition for a hospital. During and after getting my Bachelor of Arts degree I worked for a small, husband and wife owned advertising agency; an international security company; a family run, but publicly held, international packaged goods company; a privately held international packaged goods company; and a couple of other established packaged goods corporations before I started my own business (international and privately owned by moi). Sprinkled throughout is my most important job of being a wife and mother to three beautiful children and the volunteer and project perks that come along with it.

In my adventures to date, I had a sense of completion on the job (volunteer, domestic and/or professional) when I perceived that:

I was an equal and/or respected;

My feelings were as important as the facts;

Having some fun was expected and respected;

Having a family life was accepted and respected;

People around me were generally friendly, truthful, non-judgmental and I was seen as part of the team;

I was compensated fairly for the job (through pay, gratitude...);

I was appreciated;

And I was in a positive, supportive environment.

My labors became laborious and even painful to face when I knew that:

A slip of the tongue or the botch of one project would make or break my reputation (no room to be human);

I would be replaced in a blink of an eye (usually meant others were also treated poorly);

There was no room for creativity and clear cut facts prevailed;

I was not compensated fairly for the job;

The most gratitude I had for the job was the paycheck;

Having a family was viewed as a weakness;

And negativity, judgment and hidden agendas (secrets) were in abundance.

The loving and loathing ideas apply universally to being a baby sitter, minimum wage worker, domestic engineer (caring for my children and home), or working for a small business to a large corporation. In fact, national studies have shown:

Less than half of Americans in the working world are collecting a paycheck actually like their colleagues.

Only about half of Americans in the working world collecting a paycheck are satisfied with their jobs.

If you are out in the working world, look to your left and look to your right. One of those people, on average, doesn't like working with you. Workplace dissatisfaction and stress is the number one health problem for working adults. I, personally, did not like what I allowed the corporate environment to do to my personality and internal balance (or imbalance as it were). But the fact that women still don't get paid as much as men in the exact same position still baffles me. In 2002, although women make up 51% of the population and earn 56% of all bachelor-level degrees awarded (according to the U.S. Department of Education), a recent study revealed that men in life sciences (for instance) are earning almost one-third more than women (Washington, DC-based American Association of the Advancement of Science's, first study of its members). In the "2001 Census of Women Board Directors of the Fortune 1000," a report released by Catalyst revealed that women hold only 12.4% of all board seats in the Fortune 500.

Do you think you are safe from unproductive energy transfers related to these statistics if you have taken another path and are supporting your family by being a full-time mom or dad? Probably not, because your life partner can bring the unhappiness home. If you perceive that family members take you for granted, how do you address this lack of respect? How can you help them understand that running them all over town, preparing meals, cleaning their clothes, organizing family events, volunteering for school activities, scheduling doctor's appointments, doing yard work is important work? Whether you do some of the above, all of the above or more than the above, when we love who we are when doing a job others feel that energy as well. To get in touch with how to get to that place, think about the following:

I most value my "job" when...

I feel most valued in my "job" when...

I feel successful when...

I least value my "job" when...

I will minimize the pain of doing the least valued part of my "job" by...

When I cross over (no longer in my physical body), I will remember...

When I cross over (no longer in my physical body), I will be remembered most as...

How are you placing yourself one step closer to heaven on earth?

The Pessimists' Theory... Where you come from defines where you will end up...

"There is no useful rule without an exception."
—*Thomas Fuller,* M.D., *Gnomologia (1732)*

IT DOESN'T MATTER WHAT WALK OF LIFE, what your race, what your idea system, the glass can always be half full (instead of half empty) but it is up to you to create that reality. After I released my first book, *Adventures of a Mainstream Metaphysical Mom,* a reporter came to my home and said, "I'm going to be a cynic for a minute and say you have it pretty good. Why are you the expert?" I responded, "I not only have it good, I have it great! That's why my work is as much a success story for practical living as it is mind, body, and spirit focused ideas. I am that small percentage that 'felt' her way out of sexual, physical, mental, alcohol and drug abuse. I ignored the statistics. I got an education because the government had programs out there to pull people like me out of this pattern. I married a man who was the exact opposite of my abusive father. I maintained the strength that was demonstrated by my abused mother throughout my childhood (not afraid to work hard, playing and exploring a variety of subjects and places on a shoe string budget...)." Even more interesting is the fact that there was only a short time that I (with my sister and mom) sought professional counseling and it was directly after we found out that my sister had been sexually abused by our father.

I was in college and I can't remember going for counseling more than a few times and it had very little "ah ha" impact. I once attended an "Adult Children of Alcoholics" meeting and found that to be a waste of my time also. I am certainly not a doctor and I know my sister received counseling and found it to be effective. However, I was blessed with drive to improve my life, granted ignorance to statistics and was too plain old stubborn to accept others' reality. You can lead a horse to water, but you can't make her drink. It has to come from within. There has to be the inner strength that says, "Anything is possible."

When my mom began her experience with ovarian cancer, her ovary was the size of a grapefruit and she had another huge cancer mass covering her ovary the size of a football (which is the reason they couldn't see her huge ovary). The cancer began to spread to her colon by the time she made it to the operating room. I knew, intuitively, that there was no reason to fear or be in panic, but some of my inner circle were very angry with me, accusing me of being "...in denial! Why aren't you not taking this seriously?" After her operation, the doctor said, "I won't give you percentages, I'll just say that we are working toward a cure." While others were thinking about getting my mom's estate in order, I was having lunch with her while she was having chemotherapy every month (she was hungry when she got chemo... how's that for a gift?). She was at my house constantly playing with the kids, watching television, going to low stress events, eating breakfast, lunch and dinner at my house. Her vision... staying alive to see how her grandchildren turn out!

Her oncologist still shakes his head when he sees her nine plus years later and says, "You shouldn't be here." Although a poor affirmation on his part, mom broke all the cancer rules and lived. My siblings have broken the rules regarding patterns of abuse and poverty. I have lived my life breaking the rules (even my own). That's why I live by ideas. If I lived by beliefs, facts, rules, and labels you and I would never have met!

The pessimist theory continued to lose its steam when June 1997 a business was born servicing the body, mind, spirit-oriented consumer. I was a sole proprietor who worked out of my home not sure where my journey would take me but felt ready. I worked hard to get to the point of obtaining my Bachelor of Arts degree, survived thirteen years in corporate America and the glass ceiling, and, in the midst of all of this, married my life partner and had a family. I funded my business from savings and creative credit card financing. By my fifth year in business I had a warehouse to fulfill orders and manage inventory, a sales manager, and a dozen and growing sales representatives. I created a book publishing arm to compliment my wholesale company and partnered with numerous suppliers, retailers, and distributors to create an international business supplying products to retailers throughout the U.S.A., Canada, UK, Ireland and more. Utilizing my network of retail partners, I also created a service arm for authors and artists to do lectures, workshops, book/art signings and individual consultations throughout the U.S.A.

About three years prior to starting my company, I recalled having a networking lunch with a former manager who gave me no encouragement when I said, "I'm thinking about starting my own business. Do you think I can succeed?" Although a closed-ended question, I was not expecting a yes or no answer but a way to seek feedback regarding my strengths and weaknesses and some possible contacts (as this particular manager had run his own company for a number of years before re-entering the corporate world). He responded, "No." A bit dumbfounded from the lack of support, we made some small talk and I decided to go on my way. He closed our conversation with, possibly perceiving that I was seeking his approval for my vision, "I guess you could be a good business owner." While my first inclination was to counter with a cynical, "Whatever," I shook his hand, thanked him for his time and was clear that his judgment wasn't about me but about his own failures (i.e., "If I couldn't succeed in my business, how could she?"). This experience encouraged me to research, study, and seek training to increase my likelihood of success. I left stereotypes, labels, old beliefs and others' projections of who I was by the wayside. I combined my formal business training with the ability to feel my way to the next move to grow, to succeed, and to do what I loved to do. My glass was not going to be emptied by an incorrect perception.

In a mid-western city, there is an interesting dynamic going on. There is an unspoken rule that is unlike any other area I've experienced. It's a rule that (my interpretation) keeps people in "their places."

A former co-worker (not from this mid-western city but working and living there at the time) was asked by a work acquaintance, "So where did you go to school?" He replied, "I got my Masters from Northwestern and…" The acquaintance quickly interrupted, specifying, "Which high school?" This simple question helped the person immediately categorize him. In this major city, if you were a transient (relocated for work) you were only accepted in a certain area of the city. If you went to X High School then you were accepted in another community. If you went to Y High School still another. I have asked a number of other friends who live or have lived in this area (not natives) about this dynamic and sure enough they say, "Yeah, it's the oddest thing." It's odd when it's unexplainable or mysterious. I say it's just another way to quickly label, to stereotype, much like we do in the metaphysical world with astrology or numerology if the Universe of free will and choice aren't kept at the forefront of our minds.

Ask yourself, why do I label, enforce rules in my life, and when do I have unshakeable beliefs? Is it because I want to control? Is it because I need to feel safer? Be a healing force in society, in your community, in your home, in your place of employment. Understand others, while attempting not to judge. The first place to start is not to judge yourself. If you come from a poor family but are living in the lap of luxury (this is all relative… if you have food, clothing and decent shelter this can be luxury), be okay with your roots. If you were born with a silver spoon in your mouth, had all the education and things that money could buy and are living a more conservative lifestyle as a result of your choices then be okay with this as well. Don't allow other peoples' projections of where you should be create your reality or you will just be plain old stuck! You will never be happy because you feel like you need to answer to others' expectations. How can you be good enough to you? That's all that matters.

The Not Good Enough Theory... Where I come from defines where I will end up...

> *"The rich (wo)man may never get into heaven, but the pauper is already serving his term in hell."*   —*Alexander Chase, "Perspectives" (1966)*

I HAD THE HONOR OF MEETING a woman who did a lot of volunteer work for women's groups and her husband, a school teacher, who taught a number of years in lower income schools. They were exposed to numerous dysfunctional family situations that went as far as a teenage daughter being loaned to her mother's landlord (becoming pregnant at least three times before the age of seventeen) so that she and her family could continue living in their apartment. Not being able to fathom why people stay in these types of situations, she proceeded to share a story about a girl with Appalachian background who had gotten her undergraduate degree, was on her way to graduate school on scholarship and had to stop abruptly when she married and had a baby with a young man from her low income hometown. Why does this happen? She had her ticket in her hand and she threw it in the trash. Or did she?

Transitioning into high school, I really wanted to be ready for college but was concerned that my local public school wasn't going to prepare me. I asked my mother if she could send me to the private Catholic school that many of my friends (with higher family incomes) were attending. It was a struggle, but she managed to scrape up the extra money every month. I remember one of the boys making fun of me saying, "Why is an East End bum (low income area) like you going to our school?" What could I say? I certainly didn't feel good enough. My neighborhood friends would poke fun at me and say, "When are you going to stop being a snob and come to the school where you belong?" So you have a struggle on both sides. Unfortunately jealousy, labels, control, and territories create comfort levels for some… "You're the poor kid. Why are you trying to pretend like you're something you're not?" If you are having a particularly bad day you begin to ask yourself the same questions: "Who do I think I am? My true friends knew that I was poor and accepted me anyway. What was I thinking?"

My last two years in high school, I went to the local public school and my neighborhood best friend said, "It's about time you came to your senses and remembered who you are." The path to improvement, betterment, growth can be a very lonely one and you have to be willing to walk it alone. It can be very painful but the rewards are infinite. You're going to slip. You're going to have bad days. You're going to take a few steps back every now and then. But to nourish your spirit, it's necessary. And don't look back!

Who have you allowed to stop you from living your dream? Why would you allow other peoples' opinions to push you down a path that doesn't nourish your soul?

Wearing Your Principles on Your Sleeve

"(Wo)Men of principle are sure to be bold, but those who are bold
may not always be (wo)men of principle."

—*Confucius, "Analects" (6th B.C.)*

I WAS AT A VISIONARY INDUSTRY BREAKFAST and the question came up if you should use the word "New Age" in store names or descriptions. There was a major discussion about the curb appeal. Will it bring people into the store or will it scare people away (some people see New Age as the work of the devil)? What it came down to is it depends on the region. In many areas out West this was a major consumer draw, but in other areas this was taboo. My overall take on the subject is why should we hide our principles, our character, what we are, how we think, what we sell, what we buy? What are we accomplishing by pretending to fit in?

When I wrote *Adventures of a Mainstream Metaphysical Mom*, some said, "You know the word 'metaphysical' is going to scare many people away!" When a copywriter called me to talk about an ad for a radio and television publication she said, "Do people make fun of you?" (Needless to say, I decided to switch copywriters.) I've even heard that I've become an embarrassment to certain relatives as a result of my books.

Many times to express your true self, your true principles, your character, it isn't about fitting in. It's about doing what fulfills your soul and knowing that you expressed your feelings and demonstrated your true character regardless of outside pressures. Of course, there are consequences to your actions and there are ways to squeak your principles through without getting a whole lot of negative attention. Some would call this bridging the communication gap but there is bridging and there is compromising your integrity.

In a former corporate marketing job, a new peer came on board and he was ready to make a name for himself. Phillip came from a large corporation and it quickly became apparent that one way for him to get attention was to make me look bad. So as he spent his time doing his behind-the-scenes chatter, I ignored him. I did my job to the best of my ability. I didn't seek revenge. I didn't fuel the fire. And I turned the other cheek when inappropriate comments were made in company meetings. As a result, it got back to me that I was receiving some behind-the-scenes support from a couple of influential people within the company. As comments continued to fly, these key people began to put out the political fires on my behalf and his comments fell on deaf ears (or so it seemed).

Phillip was the type that just didn't give up, however. I was managing the flagship brand for the company and he wanted my job (as it turns out). As much as I tried ignoring it, the guy just got under my skin, and every now and then I would get frustrated. The problem with not strategically communicating and taking the non-emotional high road is you get stuck in the muck. The minute you participate then the pursuer has, in essence, won.

So Phillip and I were in the corridor talking to our manager and all of a sudden he said, "I know why you wear those shoes." (My favorite, multi-colored, and what I thought to be, creative shoes.) Caught by surprise and irritated with the unending comments I snapped back, "Oh really, well why don't you tell me why I wear these shoes!" Our manager quickly jumped in and said, "All right, you two." This guy, inappropriately, attacked my look. But by getting irritated, I was now part of the problem. Imagine how much energy I wasted and allowed him to capture. I wasn't as aware of the energy that came from within; a bright, warm, loving, wise, guiding light. While I did, intuitively, know that participating was a "no no," sometimes I just wanted to wring this guy's neck!

In the first "Harry Potter" movie (and book) there was a scene where an evil sorcerer was surviving by drinking the blood of a Unicorn. In this story, the Unicorn was one of the most pure animals in the forest and to live this way was for the sorcerer to live a cursed, half-life. He clung to physical life by sucking the purity and good from another. The message here is have confidence in your personal light and your inner wisdom.

Practice living your principles. If you don't know what those are, now is the time to get to know your inner self better. Ask yourself some simple questions about your principles:

When you do something as a matter of principle, are you pure of heart or doing this in anger or revenge?

What are the principles (basic truths) that you live by?

Do you live these basic truths as a result of your inner knowing and independent thinking or are they old ideas that you haven't had the courage to revise?

Wear your principles on your sleeve. Be your own hero. Be true to yourself while doing harm to none.

Physical Debt and Spiritual Practices

"Words pay no debts."

—*Shakespeare, "Trolus and Cressida" (1601-02)*

I'VE COME INTO CONTACT WITH A number of "spiritual people" who don't honor their debts. I've watched "spiritual" people literally "borrow" money from other "spiritual" people and they simply don't pay it back. What was interesting was to watch them justify their actions. An even more interesting pattern was to watch the borrowers put themselves in victim positions. This truly crushes the spirit of those who never pay the physical debt off (think there may be some non-physical ramifications?). It's a temporary blow to those ripped off unless they continue to allow others to beg, borrow and steal from them again and again.

In the United States, we take money for granted and we're given numerous options to spend money that we don't have. I, for instance, funded my business primarily through using my credit cards. As I continued to spend and pay off or, at least, pay regularly, the credit card companies became very generous and increased my spending limits to the point that I (and my company) had/have hundreds of thousands of dollars available to us.

Interestingly enough, one of the ways your credit rating is graded or ranked is by debt ratio. If you have a pool of $200,000 available to you and you have a $100,000 balance then you have a fifty-percent debt ratio. They also look at how long you've had a credit card. If you switch to a credit card with a better interest rate and cancel a card that you've used for six years with a much higher rate it can actually have a negative impact on your credit ranking. If you keep this longer-term credit card but have a small or no balance on it, you actually increase your ranking because it demonstrates more stability.

Knowing all of that, my company (and as a result I), had an uncomfortably large debt. I had a plan to pay this debt off, but there were times when I felt a bit helpless and frightened. So one day I typed "file bankruptcy" into keyword search on the internet. Lawyers popped up, organizations that could clear your debt in a week with no repercussions and then a non-profit organization came up. I went to the site to see what they had to say as I was feeling a bit vulnerable on this particular night (after looking over my books and company debt).

There was a lengthy story about a man who filed bankruptcy and how terrible his life was and continues to be even after finishing out his ten year prison sentence that basically says that he can actually have the right to credit again. Regardless, the fact that you have filed bankruptcy will always follow you because applications for, say, a mortgage or for employment ask "if you have ever filed bankruptcy" not "are your ten years up." And if you go to a non-profit organization (like a relative of mine did to get his financial matters in order), and they put you on the "one-payment" program, many look at you as a bad credit risk as well. So how do you win at this borrowing game? How do you work the physical process and maintain spiritual integrity?

Some would say, "don't spend." That is definitely an option but that's like saying, "don't have sex" to other target audiences. To abstain is usually not realistic but to change patterns to increase the likelihood of success is. So let's look at patterns that will enable healing and releasing with the intention of completing the circle and not causing pain to others (people, companies, etc.). Does this mean you have to give up all the extras all at once to pay off your debts? Some of it, maybe for a while the majority of it, but the goal is to integrate your physical debt with your spiritual practices. In theory your spiritual practices include handling your affairs with true integrity rather than "victimly" perceived excuses resulting in less than impeccable behavior.

Identify your patterns by asking yourself a few questions when barter trading or doing actual cash exchange:

When do I owe? This detects patterns of seasonality... vacationing, the end of every month...

Why do I owe? Is it entertainment, product purchasing habits, just trying to make ends meet, business expenses...?

Who do I owe? "Credit card" isn't an answer, it's who you purchased from that resulted in the debt.

How much do I owe?

What do I have to give up for good?

What do I have to give up temporarily in order to pay debt with integrity?

When will my debt be paid?

It could be ten years from now or even longer but your spirit soars when it knows that it's doing the best it can.

There are extreme physical realities that push physical and spiritual healing in other directions. If the basics (food, shelter and clothing) have been taken away, you're in survival mode and options fade quickly. How can you be sure to think through the burdens you carry in the short-term so that you don't live to regret them in the spiritual long-term?

Healing and Humble Pie

"He that humbleth himself wishes to be exalted."
—*Nietzsche, "Human, All Too Human" (1878)*

AN ASSOCIATE OF MINE DOES A SPECIAL releasing technique that combines a number of healing concepts with the ultimate goal of discovery (finding out what's holding you back) and then releasing it. So I had a big surprise when I sat in one of her classes and she asked if she could use me as a demo client for the technique. I heard that many people leave these sessions sobbing uncontrollably, so I asked my guides to stand on either side of me to protect me and to put me in a remote place to understand the emotion but to no longer feel the emotion as I did when I originally experienced it. We identified the emotion of "contempt" and at what ages this impacted me. Apparently, it was when I was twelve (this year was a blur but was the onset of puberty and middle school so definitely a contemptuous year) and sixteen years old. This was engraved in my brain as nobody in my family acknowledged my sixteenth birthday—odd, but a testimonial to dysfunction at its peak.

After this release or recognition of contempt, for the next week or so I was draining out little contempts I had left over—a Pandora's box of unsupportive relatives to work partners/associates and small events. Following this release, I was exhausted with negative thoughts and it was affecting work, play and inner peace. So I meditated. I asked my guides for a "bath." With this cleansing came a realization that the years before seeking inner peace, clarity and balance, contempt kept me alive. It was the fire in my belly—the "oh yeah, I'll show you" stuff. It helped me survive the abuse, the "injustice" (or so I thought at the time), which resulted in apologizing to my oldest daughter.

When my daughter turned ten (she calls it her double digits), I got very angry with her and her father. She wanted to spend her birthday money from relatives while I was out for the day. I agreed, as long as she didn't open any of her presents until I got home to celebrate her birthday as a family. When I got home that night, everything was open, she was wearing or playing with all of her new birthday items. I was furious with her father and my daughter to the point that I didn't celebrate her birthday the next day (actual day of her birth). Of course, what she and her father did was inconsiderate (this wasn't their original intention, but...), however my punishment did not match the crime. I was reliving the contempt I felt for my family when they skipped my sixteenth birthday. On my daughter's twelfth birthday, I let her know that I was wrong for getting so angry on her double digits birthday. She made the comment, "It's okay Mom, I'll probably do that to my kids." Eeeeek!!! I responded very concerned, "Well that's the reason why I'm telling you now. I was wrong. Let's heal that wound from my childhood and now yours."

There's lots of humble pie to be eaten during daily healing processes. Healing comes with acknowledging old destructive patterns and breaking them. This means you now label an old behavior wrong. Still to this day, birthdays are sacred days in our household. I've even been known to take my children out of school to be sure that we can celebrate the actual day of birth as a family. However, the destructive contempt pattern has been identified and minimized. Can you identify a pattern that would increase your quality of life by minimizing or completely alleviating it?

If I had a Hammer, I'd only Hammer on My Terms...

"There are people who are virtuous only in a piece-meal way; virtue
is a fabric from which they never make themselves a whole garment"
—Joseph Joubert, "Pensees" (1842)

WORKING IN A MORE CONTROLLED environment, out of my home, has made it easier to settle myself into a healing, mind, body, spirit balance. I don't have layers of bureaucrats, hidden agendas and judgments that come with large numbers of people trying to survive the rat race called a career. Wearing comfortable wooly socks, baggy clothes and no shoes and not being forced to go out into the highway traffic jungle every morning really alleviates intensity levels.

Prior to owning my own company, I worked in national brand

marketing, advertising and public relations for about 13 years—a "Type-A," fast-paced, highly competitive career. I absolutely loved being in marketing and particularly being a product/brand manager. And as I look back on my thirteen plus years of corporate experiences I realize that I was consistently looking for a personal environment and sought out companies that were independently owned. My thought process was that these types of companies would be more inclined to put people and family first. At the end of the day, we all need to pay our bills, so what does that mean?

I saw a great movie with Robert Redford. He was an army General that was incarcerated for not following orders because they didn't match his value system. When his daughter came to visit him in jail, she asked why he wanted to see her after all these years. Her position was that he did a lot of great things but he wasn't truly her father. Since most of his time was spent serving his country, she really didn't know him. As a parent striving to balance all that I love… my family, my relationships, my job and finances, my passion for writing, my studies, my physical well-being, my spirit… that would be a devastating comment from my child(ren). And yet, I still feel like this could happen. My children don't see the logic of me sitting in front of a computer during summer break or when they need attention and the needs are very different between a two-, ten- and twelve-year-old. My children label me grumpy when I'm focusing on a project for work. Taking more time away from my family, I love writing a few lines here and there, and studying new material nourishes my spirit as well. What is the right level of concentration for any particular area of life? Work takes up about one-third of our lives. Another third is spent sleeping and the other third is spent doing everything else. "Work" means anything from a 9 to 5 job to running the kids all over kingdom come for sports, school functions, doctors' appointments, etc. More accurately put, how can we be fulfilled and achieve happiness for our individual selves as well as for those around us (if this is an important element for you)?

The fact is, I didn't really have much of a grasp on mind, body and spirit balance until I started a family. Having children made me think more about my definition of quality of life. You don't have to become a parent to have this internal balance news flash but, like many parents, my vision was to make their lives as perfect as possible, so I began to wonder how I could do the same for myself.

Here's an idea… you can't be a loving, honest, happy, fulfilled person at home only or at work only. It has to go hand-in-hand. Think about it. When you're in a bad mood at work, will you all of a sudden be in a good mood when you talk to one of your children or your significant other? Some people can do this, but I don't know them.

It seemed that as I worked my way "up" into larger companies, the less soul they had. Why? Spirit was not trickled down, even in family-owned, independent companies. It wasn't allowed to. In brand/product management (my corporate career of choice), your success (and the respect you received as a result) was based on how large your product line was. So every time I was promoted or made a move to another company it was because I got to manage more money (in essence). I made a move to a privately held company (which also included a number of family members working within the company) with larger brands. Their philosophy was to do everything state of the art and plan as if they achieved the next level (i.e. buy equipment, hire employees, define processes that match the "next level"). This isn't a bad philosophy until current employees run around like scared mice because they're not feeling the spirit and have the idea that they won't make the "next level" cut. Although this wasn't the case when the company was smaller and had closer contact with the "soul" owner (I was told by some longer-term employees), layers of management were added and soul contact was limited by top management.

When we had meetings, the objectives had to be crystal clear and were (most of the time) stated up front so that the dialogue would always stay on track and be efficient (with a little spirit mixed in they could actually be enjoyable). We were actually trained on how to participate in the process effectively and educated on definition of terms so we were all on a (perceived) equal playing field. However, there were frustrating times when people would sit in a meeting arguing process and then bicker about the definitions of a Vision, Objective, Strategy or Tactic (talk about taking you off track). An extension of this company creed or success model was to have feedback sessions with all employees. The owner's goal (and, as a result, upper management's goal) was to keep his finger on the pulse of the "people," but lines between him and the "people" were clearly drawn by management layers between him and "us," and if you gave the wrong feedback you were blackballed. Although I was told by my managers that I personally "fit into the corporate culture," the Vice President of Sales was quick to give me a direct message (at a sales meeting) within a month and a half of being with the company, that being a mother and having such a long driving distance (two hours a day round trip), my choice in companies probably wasn't a good one. When he became Vice President of Sales and Marketing (I was in the marketing department) and he called me "Missy" to put me in my place, I knew my days were numbered. There was obviously a disconnect between the owner with soul and middle management soldiers jockeying for position.

So how do you integrate soul into your personal and/or professional life when experiencing these and other types of obstacles? How do you hammer on your own terms? Why do you hammer? Are you making a positive impact intellectually, physically, socially, spiritually (one person at a time)? Are you willing to compromise your values, virtues, self to get to the next level? Is it more and more and more money that you desire or to know that you have left a mark in some way? Just remember, the goal is to smile more than frown as

"*Too long a sacrifice/Can make a stone of the heart.*"
—*William Butler Yeats, "Easter 1916" (1916)*

Stop, Regroup, Recover, Resurface

"*They are proud in humility; proud in that they are not proud.*"
—*Robert Burton, "The Anatomy of Melancholy" (1621)*

I'VE MADE MY MARK BY SUPPORTING others' work, and booking authors and artists throughout the United States to do book signings, workshops and individual work. I built my company to the point that it was servicing hundreds of retail outlets, hired a sales manager and dozens of sales representatives. Then it was time to promote my new work, my book(s), my workshops. Eeeeek! I have to promote what I do personally?

My first trip to promote my book, workshops and individual sessions was in a rural area. I traveled with a friend who usually filled the room when she spoke. Even though I was known in the trade (business to business), I wasn't known by the consumer and my material was out of the mainstream and metaphysical norm. When I got to the show, a number of people were waiting to purchase my book, get it signed and chat. But reality hit when I had three to eleven people in my workshop. I say three to eleven because I started with two men (who came with their wives but left in the middle of the talk), one two-year-old boy, some came late and left early, but three women seemed to be mentally present while I shared my material.

So I shared my material with excitement looking for any reaction from the audience that would lead me to believe that I was making a difference in their lives. Within thirty-minutes, I shared too much information as I saw, even with my three "present" listeners, glazed-over faces.

Following the workshop, I reminded myself that everything happens as it should and tried to keep my chin up when my friend who filled her workshop said, "So, how'd it go?" My response (trying not to make her feel like she couldn't celebrate her success), "I had a modest, comfy group." One person that stuck it out in my first official workshop (on my own material) came by the booth and asked if I could mentor her through the process that I lectured on… She just went through a difficult divorce, was a single mom, was getting remarried and was holding the vision for major change in her life and this process could help her do that. I then did an individual session with one of the employees of the company sponsoring our visit and perceived a lift in her spirit. My lesson for the day, "Make impact one person at a time, if only with ten words."

My 10-hour drive home consisted of listening to a four-hour book on tape that would bring more clarity to my personal and professional message. I had a theology discussion about the book we completed en route and brainstormed on my teaching material with my driving companion (author and spiritual teacher). While my ego would have been jumping with joy with a standing room only presence, my material, as it stood, would not have had as much impact. Humbled yet encouraged, I spent the next several months of the fall and winter cycles getting my material up to par to resurface by Spring Equinox. As Emerson said in "Wealth, The Conduct of Life" (1860), "Nothing is beneath you if it is in the direction of your life."

When the timing doesn't seem right, how often do you slow down to get it right? When you have not stopped, how long did it take you to recover and how long? How much time, money, and/or credibility was lost by not stopping and rethinking?

Intellectual

"A good mind possesses a kingdom." —*Seneca, "Thyestes" (1st C, 380)*

Back At Ya!

"He never labored so hard to learn a language as he did to hold his tongue and it affected him for life."
—*Henry Adams, "The Education of Henry Adams" (1918)*

MY MOM AND I DECIDED TO BE AT the airport by 6:30 A.M. for a flight two hours later to save us from the rush energy that commonly takes hold in these environments. When we got to the check-in counter, it was really crowded. I said proudly, "No problem, we are in no hurry. We have plenty of time." We noticed security was checking bags by hand but with the state of affairs since the U.S. attack on September 11TH, we'd grown to appreciate the effort and didn't think much more about it. Finally, making it to the ticket counter, we found that all computer systems were down. Everything was being done by hand. Still, no sweat off my brow, we had plenty of time. We got a little breakfast before we went to our gate, we got our boarding passes at the gate (because computers were down we had to go to the gate to check in a second time) but there were numbers (1, 2, 3, 4, etc.). This was a cost cutter airline and it was their practice to give numbers as boarding passes then you got on the plane by numeric order and found a seat (rather than assigning a seat ahead of time). Still no problem... We were numbers two and three!!!

While getting boarding passes, another airline employee showed up behind the desk to help his work associate and all of a sudden a half dozen or more people from the back of the line stampeded the desk. The employee asked them to return to the back of the line. I happened to be on my cell phone giving my husband updates on what we were up to, and devilishly and a little more loudly than I should have said, "Yeah, a bunch of people who didn't listen to their parents about waiting their turns got shooed back to their spots in the back of the line."

It's the smaller things, and the humor in them, that make the biggest impact because your mind can be a bit clearer in these situations. Folks were beginning to gather at the gate to get on the plane and I, a bit indignant, said to my mom, "Why do people have to gather around an area like that? We all have numbers (and our number put us up at the front)!" When it was time to board, we went up to the front of the line and a man and woman said basically, "To the back of the line for you. We've been waiting

in line and you need to do the same." I showed them our boarding passes
(as if a trophy) and said, "We have positions number two and three." She
and her husband became red faced, more argumentative and angry so I
went to the desk and asked, "Am I in the correct line and am I permitted
to do what I'm doing?" Uninterested, the attendant responded, "You're
in the right line" and we jumped back into the line and boarded the
plane. Mom asked me what the deal was and perturbed I said, "They
were wrong and we are fine." The couple were about ten steps ahead of
us looking back, chattering and asking each other, "What did she say?"
as their eyes darted back and forth toward the plane and back to me.
Now, mind you, the passengers boarding behind us had no idea that we
were not "cutting" into the line after this altercation. We found our seat
at the front of the plane and I felt like people passing were psychically
saying "Line Cutter!"

I was frazzled after this energy exchange so I closed my eyes. I breathed
out the yucky energy and pulled in the healing energy. I brought my pulse
level back down to normal and suddenly felt myself grinning. What kind
of metaphysical poetic justice is this? I judged the potential "line cutters"
not an hour earlier and got it right back. It didn't matter who was right or
wrong as my guides threw judgment back into my face. Talk about quick
learning! Who knows how this lesson saved me from myself in future,
seemingly harmless, situations? When have you had to swallow your pride
and acknowledge your miscalculation in judgment?

Buried in the Day-to-Day... How do we understand where it is taking us?

"The best/Thing we can do is to make wherever we're lost in/Look as much like home as we can."

          —**Christopher Fry, "The Lady's Not for Burning." (1949)**

THE TOUGHEST PART ABOUT connecting with your spirit guides, angels, God, Goddess is the noise we create internally and expose ourselves to externally. With a two-year-old, a business going through a major growth spurt and two other children with individual needs (not to mention staying connected with my husband), I had convinced myself that I didn't need to get quiet for any length of time. I would dream on it and do all of my work then. My intuitive skills, after all, were getting sharper and more reliable day-to-day. But the opportunity arose when my husband was out of town for nearly two weeks and I had the bedroom all to myself. I thought, "I'll do something novel and meditate!"

I leaned back with a bunch of pillows on my comfy bed, closed my eyes and went on a trip to my "sacred place." Although I visualized this area a number of years ago, I was out of practice so I asked my guides to protect me on my trip and my higher self to come through to escort me through the process. At 12:30 A.M. and no external noise, husband snoring, children's pleas and phones ringing to disrupt the process, I slipped into my meditation quickly. My goal: to do this three to four times a week for only 15 minutes so that I didn't feel like it was going to be a chore.

I chose to get on an elevator and then enter into a portal but when I got on the elevator, I didn't see my ethereal higher self (long blurry white robes, long brown hair, and undistinguishable features), instead I met

Margaret! In more defined robes, white short hair (classic hairdo from the 40's or 50's), and very defined face, this brassy, fit but full figured woman said in an almost irritated voice, "Well, come on Michelle!" I responded, "Where's my higher self?" She replied, "You need someone more down to earth to work with now," and went on to say, "I'm Margaret and I was you in another lifetime." Surprised but feeling comfortable with this guidance, I jumped on the elevator and went to the portal but it was closed. I looked at her confused and she said, "It's not time to go in." My meditation was over, I looked at the clock and 15 minutes had passed! When I laid down in bed I thought, "Be careful what you ask for! Can't wait to see what's next!"

In contrast, a friend of mine meditates everyday for about an hour. She has a strong opinion on the difference between meditation and prayer. One is to connect with your sacred self and the other is to ask for something. Looking intensely for healing for many physical and spiritual reasons, she couldn't get to the root of the problem she had with her eyes. Usually the problem occurred when she was going on a trip to promote her work. She was very frustrated because she couldn't figure out what she didn't want to look at. I, initially, thought that she was afraid to see herself fail or (even more complex) succeed. But something she said in passing stuck with me, "Whenever I lose my sight, my other senses heighten." It wasn't until nearly a year later that I woke up with an "ah ha." When having dinner with her one night, I said, "Try this on for size. The loss of your physical sight isn't an issue, it is a solution to heightening your less used senses." It was time to abandon her "seeing is believing" philosophy so that she could evolve to the next spiritual level. That very next week, she had another promotional event and developed dizzy spells and loud ringing in her ears before making her four-hour drive. The day before she left, words formed to prepare her for the trip ahead. While the specifics aren't the point of this story, she couldn't believe the things that she was "seeing" in her mind's eye while doing her individual sessions that week-end. Her visions were incredibly accurate and astounded even her—practice, awareness and pure intention made perfect.

Another friend embraces the "living Christ" in her daily process. Her position is conceptually, "Buddha is dead. Christ lives!" You can actually feel a warmth coming from her as she talks about the word of God being communicated through the "Holy Bible." She is thrilled that she can get to know Jesus intimately before she celebrates eternal life with "Him." With excitement, she rattles off the many ways "the words" have been proven true. She has a study group that analyzes the lessons in the "Holy Bible" (called a cell group) and is in awe of this supernatural (her descriptive word) document. We truly love each other but have a different way of expressing our spirit. What I am looking forward to, however, is her promise to read my first book *Adventures of a Mainstream Metaphysical Mom,* and quote scripture in certain sections so that I can learn more about what it truly means to embrace Jesus Christ as Savior from her perspective (actually not her words but the word of God per my friend). Simply put, I am not going to experience eternal life with "Him" if I don't embrace Jesus Christ the way it is spelled out in the Bible. I'm holding the vision that she still loves me after she reads my first book and look forward to her intense study in relation to intuitive ideas with fewer rules and regulations.

On the flip side, a friend who was entrenched in the practices of new age or body, mind, spirit industry switched to intense mainstream overnight. She was tired of not being able to make ends meet, and frustrated that her efforts to sell her spirit-driven work didn't fill her financial void, so she worked 60-80 hours a week in mainstream America, leaving no time for her spiritual (creative and otherwise) expression. Once very accurate in her intuitive predictions, in casual conversations, during this stage, she would predict future events and they were off the mark. She was beginning to draw conclusions in the same way that many people do, "my small piece of the world does this, therefore the rest of the world will do this as well." Of course, the connection can't be entirely inaccurate if you buy into the idea that "All is one" but let's say you owned an ice cream parlor. Your ice cream sales were at an all-time high and there were two trends that coincided with your ice cream sales: the weather was sunny and 80 degrees or higher; attempted rape incidents increased. Does the ice cream parlor owner deduce that if she stops selling ice cream, the attempted rape incidents will decrease? If we all stop eating ice cream will rape be a thing of the past? Of course not, but you can see how we can fall into this trap.

My observations are very black and white by design and we all participate in the world to various degrees, but going to extremes creates an imbalance and imbalance creates less flexibility and less flexibility creates negative emotions that include anger and frustration. Extremes are, sometimes, easier for people. It's all laid out so they don't have to consider the gray areas. So the question is how can we manage extremes? It's connected with being okay with the adventure called the unknown. Identify your personal extremes. How can you gracefully take the good with the bad, the diverse ideas of living with the less flexible, the confusion with the clarity?

Feeling like a Victim

"Some people are molded by their admirations, others by their hos-
tilities." —**Elizabeth Bowen, "The Death of the Heart." (1938)**

IT WAS A BURNOUT MONTH and half way into it, the world's most hectic
week hit. My husband was out of town for two work weeks. My toddler's babysitter and her children were sick all week (so no help there). I
woke up at 3:30 A.M. urinating blood. I had no idea what was going on
but when asking my guides the word "bladder" came into my consciousness. By 8:00 A.M., I had all three children in my van so I could get to the
doctor to get the diagnosis (it was my first bladder infection) and medi-
cation required to clear up my condition. By 8:50 A.M., I ran the kids to
elementary and middle schools. My oldest daughter's birthday was that
weekend and I had to purchase her presents and order her cake. I was
scheduled to teach a workshop on Friday and the following Monday,
three driving hours away, and coordinated being home for my daughter's
birthday celebration for the weekend. On the way home from one of my
workshops, my tire went flat in the middle of nowhere (two hours away
from home) and my cell phone wasn't picking up a signal. Sitting in my
car a bit numb I said, "Look God, this cell phone has to work so that I
can make all the calls to get me home safely. I'm going to dial now and
I expect it to work!" I dialed my first number and voila my husband was
on the phone. Ten minutes later, a police officer pulled behind my van.
Ten minutes after that AAA pulled up and changed my tire.

As I drove home, I remembered a message that I gave the workshop
attendees before I left that day. I was preparing them for Monday and had
given them all numerology reports revealing Life Paths, Heart's Desires,

Karma Lessons, plus. I noticed that there were a number of people in the group that didn't have any Karma lessons. I reminded them that if you have five Karma lessons or none, you will still have issues on a daily basis as a result of the choices that you make everyday. Having Karma to work out doesn't mean you're any better or worse off than the next person. We all still have daily dramas.

While my life has been pretty good for the past fifteen years, I still have my rough periods. I hold the vision that lessons are as gentle as possible, but that's all relative because right about "flat tire" time, I was really feeling picked on. This feeling was almost foreign to me. I hadn't fallen into this mode in years and was surprised to find myself there. It helped me, gently, remember how others with the pattern of feeling "picked on" or "down on their luck" felt. It reminded me that knowing intuitively everything will be okay (my short time of feeling helpless on a dark highway then all things came together); everything happens for a reason (gentle lessons); having gratitude for what I have in life (my husband, the police officer, AAA, doctor getting me into her office as soon as the office opened, the fact that we have health insurance, etc.); and being empowered with choice has helped me respect, trust and value my inner self and my life gifts. The other side of victim and straight into empowerment! While difficult to swallow in the moment (at times), there was no question as to whether these were universal teachings. How can you address adversity as life lessons?

Taking "No" for an Answer

"We credit scarcely any persons with good sense except those who are of our opinion."   —*La Rochefoucauld, "Maxims" (1665)*

WHEN PEOPLE HEAR "NO," some take it personally, make assumptions about the communicator and even take it as far as questioning the communicator's integrity. Here's a simple example of an exchange I had on a business matter—or what I thought was business.

> Hello,
>
> My name is Ellen and I am writing to you to see if you might have a contact email for XYZ. I organize an event called the ABC Conference..., and I would like to extend an invitation to him to attend. I would also like to use one of his images to promote... the conference, so I need to ask permission and terms....
> Thanking you in advance for your help.
> With warm wishes,
> Ellen

> My response...

> Hi Ellen,
> You would go through TLS for XYZ communication. Thank you for contacting us. XYZ, currently, is un-available for events and we are unsure when this will change. To view our terms for XYZ images, please go to our home page and scroll down....

Please let us know how we can be of further assistance.
Michelle, TLS

Her return email...

Hello again Michelle,
Are you XYZ's official agent/representative?

My email response... Yes.

Her continued email...

...will you make sure that he sees my message about
the invitation to..., because I feel very strongly that
he should at least hear about it and make his own decision?

My email response...

Truly there is no way that he will come to your or
anyone's events (at this time).

Ellen again...

I know you said he is unable to attend any events at
present, but the conference would not be until...
    Sorry to keep asking, but my instinct is guiding me
to do so, and sometimes it can be extremely frustrating

when you need to communicate with someone, but can't find them! I do hope you understand?

   Thanks again and warm wishes,

Ellen

Knowing that she wasn't going to give up, my email response was:

I don't take anything personally. I don't have time to. This is an international business servicing over 500 retailers in the U.S. alone with straightforward, no hidden agenda, answers. I own TLS and have the skinny on all matters pertaining to anyone in my group. Consider your answer coming from the ultimate authority. Please let us know how we can be of any further assistance.

Offended by the boundaries and clarification that the answer was still "No..."

Dear Michelle,

Thank you for your very 'business like' help. I appreciate you are a very busy woman with a new baby and also being the owner, founder and author, you obviously do not want to be dealing with inquiries like my own. As a news correspondent I totally understand how business can get in the way of pleasure! So with that in mind, I will waste no more of your time, and will look elsewhere for an image to carry the energy of the... conference.

Thanks for your time with angelic blessings,
Ellen

P.S. Please pass on my love to XYZ for painting such
beautiful images, he really is a very talented man
and I am sure the angels will guide him if he is coming from his heart.

A bit irritated by the personal hit and the "doing it for the universe
how dare you treat this like a business" attitude, I decided to clarify what
she was truly irritated about (instead of blaming "no" on my personal
ability to balance my life)…

Ellen,
I'm sorry that you didn't like our answer/boundaries
and therefore have decided not to use XYZ images for
your personal project. I, personally, have hundreds of
dealings a week and have time and gratitude for every one of them. Please be aware that your straight-
forward request and balancing my personal life and
my business dealings are not related.
    We appreciate your consideration,
Michelle Payton

What Ellen didn't know is that I sent this particular talent a request
(similar to hers) and received, not only "no" from this partner but additional
comments on having major money issues and not being available for public
appearances ever again as a result of having to work a mainstream job
seventy to eighty hours per week to get his life in financial order. Given

that this was a non-profit event, she, of course, would expect this talent to bear the cost of making a trip overseas as well. We all get tunnel vision now and then as we look for ways to serve our individual needs. I'm not labeling this "bad," it's simply a natural flow at times. Sometimes we are the givers of "no" and other times the receivers. Although "no" is a very direct word, many times, personal filters can create unfounded assumptions and negative ego issues. How do you handle "no?"

The Power of One

"Men are not against you; they are merely for themselves."
— *Gene Fowler, "Skyline" (1961)*

THERE'S ANOTHER TYPE OF "NO" that expresses individuality, and when handled with grace and patience, an individual may be able to evolve this closed-ended reply into a shared vision to benefit all parties involved.

I was entering a time period that required focus, swimming against the current of others' opinions and standing alone. But the Universe gave me an inner-circle taste of how it felt to be the majority frowning on the opposition when my daughter had a bunch of friends over for her birthday. They started giving options for movies to rent for her sleepover. All but our daughter wanted to see a particular movie. We said, "Okay, majority rules!" Then I proceeded to make my daughter feel guilty because she was being stubborn and acted on her individual opinion.

The Universe wasn't done with me for dishing this out as I was quickly introduced to the need or power of one opinion overnight when experiencing a new idea from our local government. We built a house for the first time. A wonderful pond was in our back yard and we enjoyed it from every room in the back of our house. To the north, and also within our viewing pleasure, was a wooded, passive, (meaning no organized sports fields, basketball courts, etc.) public park and meadow. Great blue heron would show up regularly to hunt. Ducks and geese would entertain us throughout the day. We'd witness groupings of deer trampling through our yard. There was even a time when two hawks were battling for territory in mid-air during lunch! You get the picture. Very serene and natural while still living in suburbia.

Although the house was a bit of a financial stretch for us initially, we were moving for all the right quality of life reasons. It wasn't a larger house (than we were moving from) but it was laid out differently so we could have two offices in the house and bedrooms for each of our three children. But what really closed the deal for us was the view. However our bubble was soon popped when we received word that a local government council-appointed committee proposed filling in part of the pond allowing the city to obtain about twenty-five feet of land between our home and the water. In addition to many other modifications to the north of us, the reasoning from those working from the ivory planning tower was (and I paraphrase) it was in the general public's interest to have complete access to the public pond (needs of the many outnumbering the needs of the few). The legal fact was that we had limited rights to the public pond (even though our property line went into the water). The threat of scaring the blue heron away for an extended amount of time or possibly forever, as well as all the other wildlife (in the pond and living around it) was of no concern to them. The words, "You can't fight City Hall," crept into my mind as I contacted my attorney to find out how we could protect the pond and our real estate investment.

I was on my own. Few people were going to feel bad about one home-owner in a middle class neighborhood trying to protect local wildlife, her view and property value. I trudged forward feeling a bit like a spoiled brat on one hand and a wildlife sanctuary activist on the other. It was clear that this was going to be an exercise in perseverance. The email war began as I tried to email and "cc" all the appropriate folks to find out what kind of formal paperwork I needed to submit to make the city and council aware of my concerns. Entering unknown territory and contemplating the worst, my body, mind and spirit quickly went out of balance.

Unraveled, deep meditation was the only place to find peace. In my altered state, I asked my higher self for guidance, balance and the strength to have faith that all would work out as it should. Within the week, I received a personal visit from a city council member who strongly supported the changes behind my house and explained his position. Basically (not said but implied), "You're one person and you're being selfish" became the theme of our conversation (funny how these things get thrown back in your face in a big way when it's your turn to learn the lesson). When I asked him about the blue heron that hunt in our pond and how we should protect their hunting ground, he responded, "I've seen them too (so what)." And that was one of the first pivotal moments in this drama. He didn't see the wildlife as part of the equation. I was on my own for the moment and wasn't sure if a shared vision was possible.

I had to let go of the anger and frustration (quickly moving into contempt). Over-expressing this negative emotional condition wasn't going to solve the problem. Holding onto the negativity would only create more stress on my body and spirit and even leave a negative imprint in my home so I had to make an agreement with my soul that I wasn't going to swim upstream on this. If I didn't get the sense that city officials (as a whole) were going to hear me then I would cut my losses and not put anymore energy or time into it. Soul agreement made.

When you perceive that you're stuck in a life experience that may cause you financial and spiritual anguish, how can you maintain balance? When closure may not be achievable for months or even years, how can you conserve your energy so that you can handle the overall situation with grace?

When the Goin' Gets Tough, the Universe Steps In

"If there are obstacles, the shortest line between two points may be the crooked line." —*Bertolt Brecht, "Galileo" (1938; 1947)*

ONE OF MY CHILDREN needed to go to the pediatrician for a check-up. Synchronicity peeked its beautiful head in when I bumped into another mom, who happened to be well connected in the community, and she asked, "So how did your move (to your new home) go?" I gave a quick summary on how beautiful it was but how the city was threatening to fill in some of the pond... the blue heron hunt there.... She said, "That's interesting. The blue heron that hunt in this area actually live near the shallow stream in my back yard. Let me make a few calls and forward you information that might help."

My spirits were lifted and the Universe continued to nudge me along the very next day when I picked up a few developed rolls of film and there was one (and only one) snapshot of the Blue Heron hunting directly in the spot where the city proposed to fill the pond (demonstrated that the heron was truly hunting in the shallow waters behind my home). While armed with pictures and numerous articles on protecting the nesting and (wet land) hunting grounds of the heron as well as other migratory birds dating back to the 1800's, it wasn't enough.

It all came back to connecting with people with influence in the city government because I had no legal leg to stand on. I had to find concerned listeners on the city council. Then a neighbor/friend who was irritated by the unresponsive local papers (when she and I sent letters to the editor on this issue), gave a local reporter a lecture on how our needs were being ignored in the community and asked why "our story" wasn't being covered. Well, be careful what you ask for! In a panic, my (shy in the public) neighbor/friend called me and said, "You're the talker. Call this reporter. She wants to talk about 'our' issues with the city." This very reporter became our champion, in a sense, as this article caught the city council's attention.

Before the reporter made it to my home I said to my husband, "Wouldn't it be neat if the heron showed up today?" The likelihood of this was slim to none. It was winter and the pond was frozen. I shared the picture of the blue heron with the reporter, we walked out by the pond and talked about the issues, but I could see that she wasn't doing much writing. Feeling beaten I said, "Look, I know you need something newsworthy and there are only a few homeowners that don't agree with filling in the pond, but..." Magic! The blue heron showed up and stood tall and proud on top of the ice. I looked at the reporter in excitement and said, "The heron! This is definitely a God thing." She asked, "Have you named him yet?" Then I knew that I had done everything in divine order (without getting upset, without creating negative energy around myself, my family and home) to start the ball rolling.

The same day a city official called to say that he and the mayor of our city were forming a special interest group so that individual voices would be heard. A few days later the article was in the local suburban newspaper with the color picture that I took in my back yard and the article title included, "Saving Blue Heron Habitat...." I produced buttons with the same photo to wear at the council meeting(s) and held the vision that our position was being communicated politely and professionally but firmly and clearly. Overall the strategy was to attract people with honey rather than drive them away with vinegar.

It was quickly evident that each perceived obstacle was actually a stepping stone to get to the next level. Do you question whether you should move down a path because obstacles continue to block it? Are they truly blocks or path realignments? Ask yourself, "Does new information continue to present itself by popping into my head? Do people enter the problem-solving picture to encourage my quest?" If so, persevere and calm yourself enough to be as okay as possible with the fact that the problem will be solved at a time that will result in the most optimal results. Visualize fruit (tomatoes, peaches, nectarines, bananas) that you just purchased or pulled from your garden but they're not quite ready to eat. If you allow them to ripen in the window or on your counter then it's the ultimate sweet experience to eat.

Dreaming Your Way to Healing in the Mainstream

*"Dreaming is not merely an act of communication (or coded com-
munication, if you like); it is also an aesthetic activity, a game of the
imagination, a game that is a value in itself."*
                  —Milan Kundera, *"The Unbearable Lightness of Being" (1984)*

THREE BUSINESS DAYS (a number that I interpret as revealing magic and miracles) before the council meeting I had a dream that the pond that I so love in my back yard flooded into my home (my interpretation is flood of emotions connected with this symbol). My basement floor had a layer of water in it and the ceiling was dripping and ready to cave in as a result of all the water. I vaguely recall that my father was in my home (now passed) as an onlooker as opposed to an advisor (since I don't view him as someone with sound judgment, he now seems to just kind of show up to observe when I'm processing in dream state). Then many animals began to show up in the shallow pond in my back yard so I ran to get my camera: Two baby moose with a raccoon with its back to me (next to the moose), one black grizzly bear (who was actually talking, although I don't remember what he said), and instead of my blue heron, an egret which is a bit more petite than the heron. I couldn't get a picture of any of them because they continued to appear then disappear, then the water went back down to its original level.

Symbolically, the bear awakens the unconscious and the number two does the same. Two can be seen as a double strength or double weakness (my choice is strength). Interestingly enough, we talk about people being as grumpy as bears, but they are very fond of honey. It tames the beast, in essence, again, confirming that it's best to be the peaceful person that

I prefer to be when working through this issue. The moose is sometimes associated with feminine or maternal energy (they are often seen in marshy areas or standing lakes), which is also associated with symbolizing my mother instinct to protect the natural environment in my back yard. The fact that baby moose showed up, as you might imagine, is also significant because female moose are extremely protective of their young. I am now protecting the natural state of my back yard. Very few creatures will challenge a female moose with its calf. The, even more, interesting thing about the three mammals showing up in my dream is they were all connected (and I was consciously unaware of this). The only enemy to the moose is the grizzly bear. As the situation developed over a couple of months, this also seemed to be a symbol of the city advisory board "threatening" my current way of life. The fact that it was speaking and I couldn't remember or quite hear what it was saying seemed to give the message that they were of advisory capacity to the voting body (council) and weren't meant to have a voting voice (which council ultimately brought to their attention). The moose can outrun and out swim grizzly bears if pursued. Raccoons are distantly related to bears and are so skilled at self-defense and have adapted so well to human interference that they can live within the city (possibly the elected council members). They are very interested in water because it increases the sensitivity in their hands (when washing their food, they can better feel it). It's also about masks and what masks (or disguises) to wear to get things done to better lives (in politics you take constant zigs and zags depending on the information presented to you at that time). So my symbols decoded told me to continue to defend and protect my "territory," and attract with honey. Allowing council to wear their masks would be conducive to achieving my goal(s) of keeping our area natural utilizing the honey strategy with council (council plays many sides of the fence… support advisory board, support voting public…). Although there were a number of outstanding issues to the north of us for modifications to the public park, focusing on the pond was my charge as all the animals were connected to water. In addition, all of these animals had birthing (bear up to two years) or other cycles that took time to develop. So another message was to be okay that this would take time. This, in fact, took over two years to come to a close.

Now you may be reading this and saying, "why in the world would I spend that kind of time researching messages in my dreams? It's a way to feel like you have a bit of control, or, at least, have some additional visionary information. If you're a fan of going to psychics regularly, you may just save yourself $50 or more because you just figured out what your guides are trying to share with you (which is what a psychic does… communicates with your guides, angels, etc.). If you did see value in this analysis then you might be saying, "How in the world am I going to be able to translate my dreams that completely?" The answer is that only you can truly interpret your dreams that thoroughly. People can give you advice, but you know if it is a hit or a miss. For animal interpretations, my guides know that I run to the *Animal Speak*, book by Ted Andrews, for guidance and will also use *The Mystical Magical Marvelous World of Dreams* by Wilda B. Turner for additional symbols.

Ultimately, being individual doesn't always make you the most popular person but these valuable lessons said to me, "Sometimes the opinion of one is enough." The blue heron can symbolize self-reliance, being able to stand alone, and following your own path. When working with the heron energy, there isn't a need to compete with others or be in traditional life roles. You generally know what's best for you. Not a bad place to be.

Recall a time when you had to stand alone. How did it feel? When you've observed others taking a position that was not as popular what were your perceptions? How can you gently give and receive information that is not a majority opinion?

Allowing Things to Unfold... The art of waiting

"Time deals gently only with those who take it gently."
—*Anatole France, "The Crime of Sylvestre Bonnard" (1881)*

IT WAS A BUSY DAY. My daughter's first violin recital for middle school was at 7:00 P.M. City council met at 7:30 P.M. Whirling in the chaos of being a parent and being dedicated to a cause outside of parenting, I asked my guides to stand with me, help me keep my balance and utilize my intuition to use the most effective words to handle the situation with grace. Although we know that everything turns out as it should, I began to (again) wonder, "Is my 'vision' the right vision?" I felt a bit guilty, manipulative and "political" because all my efforts really pointed to the fact that I simply wanted my way.

For the six-year timeframe prior to this bump in the road, I'd been relatively successful at (quickly) protecting myself from negativity, hidden agendas or incompatible visions. But as a result of becoming too guarded, there was the danger of becoming a hermit not capable of mixing with mainstream. So I went to two very crowded, busy places in the same night. A room full of parents enjoying their children, grandchildren, step children, etc. wasn't really all that tough, but the city meeting got a bit intense.

We, me and about twelve of my neighbors (now not quite as alone), all sat patiently as they worked through the council agenda. However, when our areas of concern were discussed (what was being proposed in our back yards), we all tried to respect the order of the meeting (open to public comments at the end of discussions) but it was torture as matters that directly impacted each of us were discussed and we began to interject our thoughts. I knew that officials and council had heated discussions the previous night with a neighboring subdivision regarding issues in their back yards as well. So, they would likely be weary and anything that we might bring up would seem to have "conflict" written all over it—no matter what was said. In fact, the stage was set prior to the meeting when a councilman posted a message on our subdivision email saying that the council would not have time to cover our "pesky issues" at this particular meeting (the magic here was this council member, in many ways, ended up becoming a supporter later).

So our "honey" strategy was a tough sell when a number of officials started getting nasty (the kind of nasty that didn't match the public comments being made). Intuitively, I/we knew that this couldn't have been entirely about "us" and, sure enough, we later found out that there was some negative personal history between some of the "officials" and specific "public." (It didn't make it right but brought some clarity.) This made for a difficult time to say the least.

Although we made some progress as a group, I felt a bit beat up at the meeting. With all the energy coming at me (as I was the organizer and the local newspaper published the article about saving the heron hunting ground in my back yard that very week), and not accustomed to that type of energy in such quantity, I was charged up. By the time I got home (which was about 11:15 P.M.), it felt like I had injected a pot of coffee into my veins. I had gratitude for the support received by my neighbors but was a bit irritated, discouraged, offended and mentally tapped out when it came to the attacks. I couldn't find a common ground with the council members and other officials to move past the negative. It all had to do with something that may or may not happen. Allowing these negative emotions to pierce my soul wasn't going to solve anything so I had to figure out how to overcome them. I tried reading but couldn't understand a word. I tried sitting in my living room, closing my eyes, and deep breathing and that helped a little but when I tried pulling in my guides, I couldn't focus enough. My mind was in complete chatter. My head, literally, felt like it was lopsided when I was trying to find my balance. In my mind's eye, I could see a line down the middle of the top of my head. The right side was much larger than the left. I didn't know what this meant (still don't), but I did know that it was important for me to even them out. I forced myself to bed about 1:00 A.M. with my head lop-sided, feeling disoriented knowing only that I had to let it go.

Can you remember a time when you just had enough? What were some of the effective things you did to stay balanced? What were some things that made the problems worse?

Achieving Balance in an Unbalanced Situation

"Much compliance, much craft."
    —*Thomas Fuller, M.D., "Gnomologia" (1732)*

MAYBE IT WAS THE FACT that I was aware of the need to balance that brought me to a better place when I woke up at 8:00 A.M. a bit more rested and "even." I had some residual yuckiness and an upset stomach from the activities of the day before, but there was nothing to be done for nearly a month so I had to let it drift into the "there's nothing to be done at this time" category and not allow it to bring me down for the next month. No sooner did I let it go, I received a call from a city official asking that I set up our special interest committee three weeks later and the affirmation from their side saying, "We know that we can come up with resolutions that all will be happy with."

To keep myself in balance, I held the vision that, "All is well in my world. All will come together for the good of all involved." I realized that this wasn't as much about formal politics as it was the politics of life. Each neighbor took positions on matters and some handled it with grace and others threw themselves into emotional trauma. At the same time, we were truly "one." The question was how could the "one" create an energy that moved forward with mixed value systems. In my world, I was talking to my guides, visualizing healing light, creating mantras, affirmations, and the like. But was this effective in a mainstream drama with so many people outside of my circle, consciousness "language" and approach?

The day arrived and about twenty people entered my home to talk about the plan behind or near our homes. Three council members (including the mayor), the city manager and the architect were all in attendance to listen to our concerns. My inner voice played a song over and over in my head. I heard Joni Mitchell singing, "Pave paradise, put up a parking lot." One of the advisory committee members, during a heated discussion, decided to propose a parking lot in our subdivision as well. My interpretation was that she was demonstrating her power over the "public." And sure enough, at our neighborhood meeting one month later, a parking lot did, in fact, make it on the plan. I acknowledged the divine humor of my inner voice tipping me off and knew that this was given to me so that I wouldn't blow my cork when this information showed up on the plan presented to a couple dozen neighbors and city officials. So, it seemed my consciousness world and practices benefited me by keeping me "level headed" and balanced.

After so many meetings, it was imperative to come up with a win:win for all parties. While the details and legal terms were quite boring, we kept it soul simple! Council and the city officials recognized the benefit of compromise but the process still wasn't over. Has being impatient ever benefited you? How can you consciously divert your attention to encourage patience?

Fed up with Mainstream Drama?
Finding a balance point through "Ready-tation" vs. "Meditation"

"Power doesn't have to show off. Power is confident, self-assuring, self-starting and self-stopping, self-warming and self-justfying. When you have it, you know it." —Ralph Ellison, *"The Invisible Man" (1952)*

WHEN I STARTED MY OWN business seven years ago (as I write) I thought, "NO MORE POLITICS." No more hidden agendas, no more game playing. But what I found out is life takes on this political role in many different ways. It doesn't take careers and finances to create these life games (take a look at the way children play).

It was kind of fun (in an odd way) to watch our local government at work. Sitting in their executive chairs at the front of the room, seven individuals sit listening to public positions and recommendations and then they vote yes or no. While, at first, our neighborhood demonstrated a united front, people began to chit chat. "Why wasn't I invited to the neighborhood meeting?" "I didn't really agree with what we said in the meeting (even though I agreed at the meeting)." "We weren't given enough time to read over the meeting notes to say whether we agreed or not...." In a public meeting that followed our neighborhood discussion, positions were changing, petitions were being circulated, the volunteer advisory committee to council was in full battle gear and decided to attack our neighborhood meeting notes.... It was a negative free for all. But it was time for me to draw a sanity line in the sand. It was the middle of the winter cycle and I was doing entirely too much socializing (or anti-socializing as it was turning out). I was quickly getting worn out and fed up with the mainstream drama(s).

The beat went on with more meetings to attend, legal departments to debate with, attorneys to get involved... feeling tired, beaten and ready to run the other way... Wait a minute! What if I did? Who would care? Would it change anything?

I needed a quick answer because I felt myself falling and fast (again)? I scribbled out a quick look on the positives and negatives of my Financial, Intellectual, Physical, Social and Spiritual areas of life to see what was out of balance. The answer at that moment was spiritual. So it was time for me to sit with my spiritual guides and have a little discussion but I was exhausted (a too familiar state for me). It was time for bed.

I walked up the steps to my bedroom and said in my head, "You know guys, I need a way to get to you fast. It's a waste of my time to lay down and totally relax my body, feel my toes, my knees... hear my heart and breathing... I want to get to you fast. Give me a direct line tonight." My husband was in bed making his heavy breathing sounds (others would call this snoring) but I didn't want to get up and find a completely quiet place. I asked my guides to help me manage the sounds and turn it into white noise (I wasn't connecting with music while meditating during this period).

I imagined, Margaret (a guide) was on my left and a warrior/(then) shaman on my right (another guide). They picked me up (by the arms) and took my ethereal self to a dimension directly in front of me. The process changed even more as we no longer stepped into an elevator (my former process of going deeply into my subconscious or superconscious) but merely took a few stairs up then walked on a short landing to get to another few steps to the portal where I could see my peaceful place complete with ancient woods and rippling water with gemstones glistening in the mild warm sun. It was like a soft black curtain or veil that covered up the entrance to my sacred world. My hand moved forward to lead me into my space and then pushed on a clear, watery, spongy barrier. And I found that I wasn't going there today. My guides grabbed my shoulders and we, as if by the speed of light, wooshed to another entrance. I'd taken long walks to this place from the rippling water entrance but I was fast-forwarded to this space and through the portal I saw a familiar grassy hill. Then it changed shape into an Aztec or Mayan pyramid but continued to be covered with grass and dirt. It was almost like it finally took shape. I walked into the portal briefly and looked around and knew I would be back later when it was time. My awareness turned to my physical body. I could feel it in a bit of a floating state. I felt safe with my guides and decided that in order for me to accelerate spiritually, I needed them with me for guidance as well as protection. They brought me back to my body (this is what I visualized) and I opened my eyes feeling a bit more connected to spirit which created more balance and I was ready to go to sleep.

One of the frustrating things about meditating or visualizing is the idea of or programming that says remaining completely still, no interruptions, keep the eyes closed at all times, etc., is a must. What I found in this "ready-tation" is that I even opened one of my eyes slightly by accident and still found myself in "spirit mode."

The answers that I received while combating my frustration is that I realized we are all capable of visiting our soul, sacred, peaceful places without being stereotypically New Age. I've experienced great results with the following:

1. Announce to your ethereal guides that you are ready to experience spirit but deep relaxation techniques are not necessary.

2. To ground yourself in the moment, envision golden or white light pulled in through your nose then out through your mouth or nose (which ever you prefer). As the golden or white light comes out of your mouth see the black speckles of negativity coming out with it and being sent to (your) heaven for healing. Do this until you can't see black specks any longer or see very few. This helps you clear out the gunk of the day, week, month...

3. If you can, while breathing, breath out the stresses of the day. Try to name them. Also acknowledge the growth that you've made for the day... "I had compassion for... I made 'x' sales, I walked fifteen minutes..."

4. When you're ready, pull in all colors or multiple colors in through your nose, down to your toes and up through your entire body (even your fingers and top of head) and out your mouth or nose (your choice). Don't over think the colors just use this as a final cleanser like when you have sorbet before a really good meal to cleanse your pallet. You could stop here to simply clear out the gunk for the moment or move to step five.

5. Imagine guides on your left and right sides. It can be angels, guides, Jesus, those who have passed on, your higher self... but don't struggle with seeing or naming them. They could just be shafts of light.

6. Imagine them actually taking you by the arms (on each side) and leading you to your sacred place.

7. Imagine your sacred place is directly in front of you and is merely covered by a veil. Step out of your physical body (see a cord connected to your ethereal and physical bodies) and literally step through the veil onto a platform then step into your sacred world.

8. Once you get there just allow yourself to let go and imagine the situation. Keep your protectors with you at all times unless they tell you specifically to do something without them next to you. Allow yourself to imagine this.

9. If you have an intention, goal, or issue, sit down and discuss it with your guides for a short time but don't put too much pressure on yourself to be there for an extended amount of time. If you're there just to build and get to know your sacred space that's okay too. Celebrate that you are there with such ease.

10. Come back (to your physical body), the same way you came in. And celebrate the ease of your journey and the connection with your spirit to create balance in all things.

I've gotta tell you. I was really pleased with this outcome. No music, no pressure to feel like if I had a tickle or itch that I couldn't scratch it, if I had a kink in my neck I could move it... just take me away! After two days of ready-tations for about fifteen minutes I felt reconnected and got back to a space of "now why was I worried or concerned?"

How the Universe Rewards being Cocky

"Here's a good rule of thumb:/Too clever is dumb."
—Ogden Nash, "Reflection of Ingenuity,"
"Verses from 1929 On" (1959)

WITHIN THE WEEK I was so relaxed ready-tating that I got cocky. I had this great new process that anyone in the mainstream or metaphysical could do! How clever was I?! My husband snored particularly loudly and was sleep jumping the night of my big adventure so I thought, "I will really put this to the test!" I was being a bit silly and said, "Hi Margaret (looking even younger this night). Hi Chief (shortened his name). Let's get rolling." We stepped directly into the veil and the portal to my familiar sacred area was open. I stepped in and asked my guides if they were coming and Margaret responded, "You know this area really well. You'll be fine on your own." I saw a translucent white cape on the ground where I usually sit and I put it on. I briefly wondered what the cape was about but was too interested in reacquainting myself with the waterfall, the dolphins, the woods, my sitting area with the large ancient tree. The cape slipped off and I'd pull it back a few times. And I was almost slap happy. I found myself testing the waters and going in and out of my ready-tation just to prove that it could be done (scratch my nose, open my eye slightly...) and in my folly all of sudden, THUD! My ethereal body slammed back into my physical body so quickly that my body actually leaped off the bed and I gasped for air as if someone had held a pillow over my face.

Okay, I was a bit cocky. While I was giddy getting re-acquainted with my sacred area, "they" added a new symbol to the mix, the cape. It seemed that this was a cloak of pride. The fact that it was clear would say that it was positive, pure, clear, and with no ulterior motives. White symbolized purity, perfection, and holiness. It slipped off to get my attention and increase my focus but I was being too clever to observe the guidance. While I'm convinced that we don't always have to be Yogi's, achieve the lotus position, or be completely still to connect with our spirit, there are limits to what your physical body can withstand. Going in and out of your body so many times in a fifteen-minute time-period can stretch you to the limit. Know that you don't have to look like you're playing Chinese freeze tag to achieve connection but don't turn yourself into a human yo-yo, either.

It makes me grin when I see this, but there is actually scientific back-up on the benefits of meditation and was reported in *Time* magazine August, 2003 in an article called "Just Say Om." Additional *Time* articles relating to this subject date back, at least, an additional fifteen years (rather than my quoting the obvious benefits you can purchase these articles directly from *Time* magazine for a nominal price). But do it for fifteen minutes, or do it for hours. Going within can benefit you in many ways with the ultimate result of finding your center so that you can act on daily life experiences with a clear head.

Ask yourself, with any type of soul connection process, why am I doing this? Is it because it's all the rage or am I looking for a place to clear my mind, talk to my higher self, research past lives, communicate with God, ...?

Getting to Know your Guides... Reaching the magic within, without floating heads

"Ideals are an imaginative understanding of that which is desirable in that which is possible."

—Walter Lippmann, "A Preface to Morals" (1929)

ONE DAY MY HUSBAND referred to himself as a "muggle" when I was explaining a new idea to him. For those who have not been exposed to the "Harry Potter" series (books and movies) this word refers to people who have one or both parents that don't have magic background. So my husband labeled himself as not capable of achieving magic. But with magic comes faith in whatever source that gives you strength. How can you access this?

When you are on the threshold of feeling (and acknowledging) the magic within, you may notice and begin to work with:

1. Ringing in your ears—my ears never stop ringing and change pitches when I should pay attention to a thought, what someone is saying, or simply get up and see what my toddler is into.

2. Flashes of colors (I see a neon lavender regularly) that blink in and out quickly, float in the air and/or show up as straight lines of colored light.

3. Shadows or blurring at the edge of living things—you're beginning to see aura activity.

4. People that have crossed over hanging out in your dreams (sometimes just in the background watching like a movie).

5. You get messages from two to three different sources in the physical about the same subject to confirm an idea or direction—your Source is giving you the signs you are looking for.

This is your personal evidence that you are being communicated to from your Source(s). The question is can you be okay with picking up on subtleties to take you in a particular direction? And can you embrace this as magic within?

I was in a very creative year during a particular winter cycle. Everything that I was doing was leading up to the spring equinox. I was writing numerous articles for magazines and publications, working on this book, running an international wholesale business and enjoying my family. Since I lost my babysitter (for my toddler at the time), I decided to make phone calls when she went down for a nap and do a lot of my detailed work between 10 P.M. and 2 A.M. When hubby was in town, I slept in for an extra hour. If he wasn't in town, after about two or three days of this schedule, I would end up napping with the baby to catch up on my sleep.

But even with the quicker ready-tation process, I didn't always feel like experiencing sacred areas. Sometimes I simply wanted to get to know my guides better and just talk to them as I lay in the non-descript nothingness. So I would do the white or golden light breathing then take the last deep rainbow cleansing breath and visualize the rainbow touching every part of my physical body to clear out any junk. The goal here was simply to forget about tasks that needed to be done the next waking day, relax and be in the moment. Following this step I would ask my current guides, Margaret and the Chief (at that time), to come hang out on my left and right and I would just discuss the day. Mostly they'd listen, as opposed to discuss, then I'd have gratitude, discuss the lessons and notice things about them as well. Like one night, Margaret became younger. Another time I was trying to make out the tattoos or painted designs on the Chief's arm. Still another night, out of the blue, the Chief decided to speak but it wasn't in broken Indian but plain old English (blew my stereotype all to hell). This is a great exercise because you're having quality connection with your

guides, angels, Source, higher self, spirit, etc. but not feeling like you need
to turn it into a journey. It's kind of like having tea and relaxing.

These are relaxing visualizations and bonding experiences with my
ultimate inner circle. A great way to get to know those completely focused
on my higher good. No mumbo jumbo struggle, just a really nice way to
blow out and review the day, connect with spirit and drift off to sleep.

Meta-tip... If you can't connect with other divine entities during
your visualization, start off just talking to yourself (like you would do in
prayer). Eventually visualize shafts of light or whatever symbolizes divine
entities to you. Over time, they will begin to take shape, communicate
in a way that's effective to you and over even more time, they will change
as you change.

Out of Control when Seeking Control

"To understand is to forgive, even oneself."
                            —*Alexander Chase, "Perspectives" (1966)*

AFTER SEVEN MONTHS, we finally made it through the first series of meetings regarding possible renovations in our back yards. This was a bit of
a contradiction in terms given that the political process is never really final.
While on one hand I was relieved that private property owners were considered as having valid concerns, it was not easy to block the "them" and "us"
energy in open forum. Certain participants within the process didn't
grasp the concept of letting go. When homeowners voiced opinions, some
interpreted them as direct attacks and it got ugly on a regular basis.

The core issue with those lacking the ability to let go was the need
to have control. It doesn't matter what the situation. Whether protecting

your property from business, government or planting a few flowers that might drape into your neighbor's yard, situations can escalate and become a misplaced way for people to perceive they have control over their lives. They're looking for ways to have a sense of power.

A workout partner was having a particularly difficult day, so I decided to focus on my workout and socialize less to give her a little more space. Finished pondering, she asked a rhetorical question, "Do you think it's important to get along with your neighbors?" I, personally, like to know and get along with a couple of my neighbors. They don't have to be my best friends but being neighborly creates nurturing energy, so I chose my words carefully since I wasn't sure where she was headed. She went on to explain that she had lived in her home for ten years and had some major problems with one of the next door neighbors. They had a few mild incidents but the big blow up was a result of planting flowers close to their adjoining property lines. Following this incident, she felt isolated, and even discussed selling her home.

Again, we see the politics of life aren't too terribly different from a city council meeting. The formal difference is there usually is a process to work out grievances or give feedback on a particular issue(s). Metaphysically speaking, letting go is a regular focus for those overcoming patterns that don't serve them or don't result in happiness. It's highly likely that you would look and sound like a raving lunatic if you talked about universal ideas in a public mainstream forum. So, the question is how can you take the high road and acknowledge the universal flow of events which ultimately leads you down the path of well being?

If you're feeling stuck, ponder the question: "The universal energy seems to be pushing in this direction. How do I fit or not into this specific picture?" Do the steps I'm taking make intuitive sense or (if I can be honest with myself) am I feeling out of control and fulfilling a sense of power for myself while hurting others? What is truly out of control in my life and am I projecting that frustration inappropriately? If I am projecting inappropriately, I'm not solving my core problem(s). In fact, I'm making myself look foolish and compiling more problems for myself.

Hey, nobody said being honest with yourself was easy. I can make my face turn red recalling some of my projections from over twenty years ago!

So Why Was I Worried? What patience and winter have in common.

"Patience and diligence, like faith, move mountains."
        —*William Penn, "Some Fruits of Solitude" (1693)*

A NOTHER MEETING. More discussions. More concessions. When would this be over? When could I stop worrying about the chain of events?

It was attorneys, engineers and surveyors time. We all gathered in my home along with my affected neighbors (which included me) whose property dipped into our beloved pond. As we hashed out the details, my neighbor (with her bionic ears) overheard one of the engineers say, "You can't (destroy the natural habitat and) fill in the pond because...." He went on to explain the problems it would cause for the community... We quickly realized that the architects never consulted the city engineering department to find out the true costs, logistics and actual function of the pond in question before proposing to fill in part of it.

We spent endless hours and months defending the position of not touching the natural landscape behind our homes. They could fill in part of the pond but they would have to dig out another side of the pond so that it would continue to serve as a flood management system and those dollars were not budgeted by the city.

There was a day when I would receive information like this and not be able to hold back the "na na na na boo boo's." But being the metaphysical follower that I am, that would just set me up for a negative cosmic come back. We handled so much of this with grace and teamwork (my neighbors and I) that it would have been a shame to wash all the time that everyone put into the process down the drain. It became clear that the city would declare eminent domain as a result of this new information (would force us to sell our land at a "fair" price so that it could be used by the public) if we didn't come to a meeting of the minds. While I did my share of worrying, I thanked the Universe for giving me the personal strength to decrease my stress level sooner than later.

Patience related to dormancy is the energy that the winter cycle of the earth creates. The winter cycle (particularly in areas where the seasons change) forces people and nature to slow down and even stop. It's a time of taking in information and forming ideas but not necessarily executing them. If you've executed ideas during the winter cycle, there's a high probability that it would take longer to execute than during any other cycle of the year. It doesn't mean that you can't create in winter (as this can be a very creative time for me personally). It simply means patience is a key factor for completion. This is a time when we notice a lot more colds, viral infections, and low energy for those who don't observe winter and patience. What do you do with this type of energy?

I was in a major creative period during a winter cycle. I created two new card lines, turned in five industry articles, completed a major portion of writing a book, and created all my workshop materials for the year as well. However, these seeded ideas were not published, finalized, or on the lecture circuit until spring equinox and beyond. There was less of a struggle because I followed the natural energy flow.

So when patience is an issue, think winter! Both are very difficult concepts, as people fight timing (especially when it's slow) and what they see as stifling energy when in fact it is a time of steady, powerful growth. People want to know when events will begin and end. They want the "known" but 'tis not the season.

How much excessive worry do we create over things that may or may not happen? And if the worst does happen, how much additional torture have we put ourselves through along the way? What does that do to our quality of life in all other areas? We feel uncomfortable with change and not knowing in general. How can we cultivate patience? How can we observe and appreciate the beat of winter?

Teaching Old Dogs New Tricks

"I can't think of anything better to do with a life than to wear it out in efforts to be useful to the world."
—Armand Hammer, "Hammer" (1987) with Neil Lyndon

ONE NIGHT MY GRANDFATHER (my mother's father), who crossed over about twenty years prior to this dreamtime visit, had me over to his home on the other side. Giving you a little background on my grandfather: he was a bigot; heavy drinker; opinionated; had guns stored all over his house (becoming a danger to others and himself by the end of his most recent physical life); was as stubborn as they come (first generation American, strict Lutheran, spoke fluent German until about sixteen

years old); extremely generous with those he loved; was my pen pal growing up; never missed my birthday (always sent a card).

On the other side, my grandfather still lived in his conservative little
home on Platt Road in Ann Arbor, Michigan but he updated it (which
symbolized new ideas and growth)... new Corian counters, clutter free,
pillows and sacred (Buddhist-like) ritual tools in the living room. Grandpa
looked familiar enough so I could place him in this physical life, but he
was slim, toned, standing up straight, had a crew haircut but his hair was
now black. There were still some areas in his home that weren't quite
updated, particularly the family room that was used a lot when Grandma
was physically alive. Grandma took care of my brother and me in this
particular room when we were young. It was her space. This room was
no longer accessible and had no steps in this dream.

I tried to talk with grandpa but he didn't respond. However, he did
go into the living space where he watched television the last years of
his physical life (the television was gone now) and knelt on his pillows
and began to pray in another language in front of a smoking bowl. No
other idols were present. Perhaps he was studying and practicing another
"religion?" Grandpa, as my mother explained it, stopped attending church
after he was no longer under the care of his parents, but on Good Friday
he would never eat meat.

Grandpa demonstrated that he had broken some old patterns in his
previous physical life and was sharing his new tricks which obviously
resulted in his peace of mind. After our Grandma died (on my first
birthday), my mom said that, "Daddy just seemed to be lost after that.
He really never recovered." However, this dream would say the physical
chains that limited him in his most previous lifetime are no longer a
factor. The question is, wouldn't it have been great to live some of this

out in the physical so as not to waste twenty earth years? Yeah, I know "they" say that there is no concept of time on the non-physical plane but it feels very real to me this very minute!

So how do you learn new tricks that catapult you to the next level of physical and spiritual bliss? What is making you unhappy? Try getting rid of that first and notice how the positive energy begins to flow. Do it now or do it later.

Practical Goal Setting

"We have two lives,. . .the life we learn with and the life we live with after that."　　　　　　*—Bernard Malamud, "The Natural" (1952)*

WHEN WE DECIDED TO BUILD a home, it was very scary. We decided to take our chances and move once our new house was finished (as opposed to selling our existing home and renting an apartment). This meant that we would be making two house payments for a (hopefully) short time. This risk was worth it to us because:

1. We weren't doing this to keep up with the Jones' but to create a more sacred space for all members of our family (believe it or not, we had some neighbors by the name of Jones).

2. We would utilize the same amount of square footage of our existing home, just move it around so that

— We both (my husband and I) had offices with a door so our kids could play without disrupting our work

— We had separate bedrooms for each child

— Our bedroom was on the same floor as our children for peace of mind for our children as well as ourselves (with an infant at the time)

3. We would live in a more natural setting (pond, woods…) with a bit more land but enjoy the security of an established suburb.

While our goals were clear, certain stressful situations would temporarily blind our direction. And one night in a huff I said, "Why are we moving?" My then eleven-year-old chimed in, "Because we want a better quality of life. We all get our own rooms, you have offices with doors and we can play more inside." The huff became a hush as I was given confirmation from the mouth of my babe. This is when you know your life is on track, when your children can play your goals back to you simply, clearly, with confidence and understanding.

While it's one special gift when kids can repeat your goals, what if they need counsel so that they can actively practice goals for themselves? All of my children are bright (of course) and have the gift of gab (imagine that), but my middle child was very "popular" among his peer group and it was beginning to adversely affect his grades. He would get good grades but his teacher would consistently ask him to expand on explanations of his work, and his handwriting was sloppy when he got lower grades than he was capable of (which meant he was rushing or racing his classmates). So how do you advise a nine-year-old how to perform to his full potential?

He was mortified when I put a goal sheet together for him and sent it to his teachers and asked him to post this on a book where he could see it everyday. He tried to negotiate with me ("Mom, I promise I'll do better!") and then, of course, he got angry ("Mom, you are embarrassing me, please don't do this!"). I may have mentioned this before: I'm okay that my kids will not agree with, at least, 75% of what I do to make them more responsible adults. My goal was clear, to redirect an extremely bright, enthusiastic, charming young man's energy and creativity so that he could be all that he could be.

So, I tried to put it as simply as possible. I made a "To Do" list for my son with the following information on an index card:

Take your time when doing your work.

Remember: You know the material and have plenty of time. When your writing gets sloppy, you're not taking your time.

Stop, look and listen, when you are tempted to talk and it's not your turn. Remember: Stop. Take ten deep breaths.

Respond completely when doing your class work.

Remember: Answers like "It was good" or "I liked it" don't answer the question. Talk a whole lot but do it on paper.

I made copies for his teachers, gave him and my husband a copy and I regularly asked him, "What are you supposed to be doing at school?" He'd roll his eyes and paraphrase his school goals. I received a note from his core teacher regarding my son's goals.

"... I continue to be impressed by you and your family's caring for each other. His "to do" list certainly has three large tasks: taking his time when doing his work, not blurting out (paraphrasing) and responding completely and listening. ...perhaps you'd consider patenting HOW this works, and think about consulting with teachers and families!

To measure Alex's overall success with only those three things would not be fair to him, because when compared to his peers many of them appear to be (probably are) much calmer. BUT, when compared to many of his peers I want you to know that he is superior in his acts of kindness, his empathy and in his compassion for others. He continues to demonstrate a wonderful blend of enthusiasm and desire to apply his learning to real life...

Thanks for all you do every day with your family... it sure shows in school!"

Partnering with those who care for and teach our children during the majority of their waking hours can only end in complete success in life. Is there a more powerful gift that you can give to your child?

But the real question is, did this process work for my son? Within a month of sending his "To Do's" to school, my son got a behavior report sent home and I saw it just by chance when I walked by as he was playing video games after school. His face dropped as I picked it up and read... "Write in thirty words or less how you demonstrated poor behavior?" He quickly interjected, "I didn't want you to see that. I wanted to show it to Dad!" But as I read down to the last question, "What are you going to do to change your behavior?" He wrote, "Pay attention to my 'To Do's' list." So, he was empowered with an answer that wasn't meaningless words like "be quiet... don't talk... do 'better'..." In my humble opinion as a mother, very powerful for a nine-year-old boy. It wasn't to say that we didn't still have some heavy discussions that night and create more notes to the teacher which resulted in an angry young man wishing that he had chosen another mother in this lifetime. But I was sure to remind him that this was his choosing. Everyone in his life is a part of his birth choice (an empowering idea that we embrace in our household) so be okay with this and let me do my job. I reminded him that I'm not punishing but insuring that when he is an adult he can take care of himself, hold down a job, and reach his full potential in school without my constant supervision.

Time will tell, but I know that I'm doing the best that I can with the information that I have this minute. How can you simplify your goals so that even a child can recite and understand them?

Physical

"It is better to wear out than to rust out."

—Richard Cumberland, Quoted in George Horne's
"Sermon of the Duty of Contending for the Truth" (1730-92)

How Symbols Manifest your Dreams

"But a man who doesn't dream is like a man who doesn't sweat. He
stores up a lot of poison."   —"The Grass Harp" (1951)

T HE WOMAN WHO USUALLY CUT MY HAIR had pneumonia so I found
someone to cut my hair in time for a family photo session. I didn't
know her so it made "hair talk" a lot of fun as I looked around
at her décor (in deep greens and beiges which is unusual for a hair salon),
spectrum lights as opposed to fluorescent and cubical walls for privacy for
each stylist. As we talked I asked her if she felt drawn to any particular
color to see if she was the green fan (wood element color from a feng shui

standpoint). She also revealed that she loved wearing black (symbolizing water and career) which fed the wood surroundings and she also owned the salon. It was fun to see how it all fit together and I mentioned to her the balance that she intuitively created within her work environment. By the time our forty-five minute session ended, I learned a lot more about her, including that she had a monogamous, long-term relationship but I didn't notice anything in her work area (hair cutting station) that identified with this until we went to the cash register. In the relationship corner of this little office area she had a picture of a famous couple that she felt were perfect together. I got a bit more nosey (I couldn't help it; by now I knew where she went to high school, where her father lived, his extended second family and what she was going to do for the upcoming holiday!) and said, "When did you put that photo in that corner symbolizing your ideal relationship?" She said, "About three and a half years ago." I said (now knowing the name of her significant other), "When did you start dating Martin (fictitious name)?" She responded, "About three years ago." I couldn't help myself responding with a grin, "So you put the most perfect, loving couple (in your opinion) in your relationship area in your cash collecting and appointment making area (a highly trafficked area in her salon) and now you have a wonderful relationship." Her response, "You know, we have to do lunch sometime!"

It's fun and harmless to test your latest training, spiritual hobby, personal theories or ideas in a neutral, safe place. So try this theory on for size: what happens when you put a symbol in an area where you see it everyday and it communicates love, stability, excitement, and deep commitment to you? You begin to visualize this world and what it would mean when it materializes for you and it can become a physical reality. Funny enough, she accidentally threw the picture away (possibly correlating with the thought that her love life was garbage or a waste) and then went rummaging in the trash to find it so she could frame it! Now her steady is going to family functions (and this was a big step for her, as I found out, as she made it a rule not to take run of the mill dating material to meet her father). Are there wedding bells in her future? Only time will tell, but she has experienced the love that she associated with this picture.

When I was trying to get pregnant for my third child, my sister let me borrow a really odd mask that friends passed onto others holding the vision of pregnancy. The mask was only passed on when this goal was achieved. In fact, I held onto this mask until I gave birth! The imprint was on this object for those who chose it as a sacred tool to manifest their fertility dreams.

This is very mainstream safe as no one has to know what you're up to. There are a number of symbols you can plant in your home, office, automobile (a piece of fabric on a table with symbolic colors, a coin underneath your desk mat, a picture of a person that symbolizes something you hold the vision of manifesting). Visualize something small and harmless for yourself. It doesn't have to be in a feng shui corner. Just put it next to your bed and wake up to it every morning saying this is what I visualize for myself. Cut a picture out of a magazine, download it from the internet, draw it (if you're talented in that respect), etc. Once it manifests and you see how easy it is, try something else. Date the symbol so you know when you activated the vision to find out how long it takes you to experience your own magic. Add an affirmation to give it more goal-power and clarity. Some set timelines on things to manifest (three months or weeks or...), but don't frustrate yourself by putting yourself under a timeline that may not be suitable for you. The key with this process is patience.

When You Can't Help but Care About What People Think

"Do not judge, and you will never be mistaken."
—*Rousseau, "Emile" (1762)*

IT'S DIFFICULT, AT TIMES, to remember that it doesn't really matter how others perceive my path. If I care too much about how others perceive me and what others project on me as a result it can push me back. For instance, when going back to a high school reunion or bumping into someone that you knew many years ago, how do you feel? If you've gained weight, do you feel like you're being judged for letting yourself go? If you are much more together now, do you feel like that "less than" person from the past? Who's fault is it that you feel the way you do? Your own.

When my first book came out, I found my journey paralleled many others but I also found myself (at times) almost apologizing for the word "metaphysical" in the title. But since "we are all one," how could our journeys be that much different when we all come from the same Source?

A family member was sure that his/her name was going to somehow be tarnished in relation to my work. He/she drew conclusions before reading the book and eventually "browsed the book in detail" to confirm the terrible injustice, but there was nothing to be found. However, the biggest Universal slap in the face was that I would be accused of slandering anyone for personal gain, particularly with someone I've known all of my life.

First I experienced anger. Then I removed myself entirely from the situation knowing that this wasn't about me but issues that this family member has never been able to face and I was the most convenient target. When the holidays rolled around tensions began to build as the supportive "middle (wo)man" of the family tried to coordinate how to spend time with both my family and "the others." Trying to swallow my pride, and feeling bad that this struggle was beginning to affect many other relationships, I sent an email invitation for our traditional get together then followed up with a phone call when I heard through the grapevine that a phone call "would have been nice." Relieved that my messages were received, I could say I attempted to make contact. The holidays had come and gone and I didn't have to take another look at this for a little while.

This was a pivotal point in my life where I became absolutely sure of one thing: it's healthy for me and my family to spend time with people that support our personal, professional and spiritual growth. My spiritual job is to make sure that I don't carry negative energy that will clog up or slow down my expansion.

However, I too have judged too harshly in my past, present and will in my future. When I did, I can tell you that I ended up eating my words and back peddling to those I gossiped to when the judged person(s) demonstrated kindness, integrity or other honorable qualities.

I had lunch at a nicer restaurant one day with my husband (when the cash was flowing and we had only one child to feed and struggle with during a meal). I took a bathroom break and when I came out of my stall, a woman was working on her hair, make-up, and smoothing down her clothes… spending a whole lot of time making sure everything was in place. I quickly observed myself in the mirror to demonstrate how silly it was to make such a fuss (females can be very catty and I had the "woman edge" that day) until I saw her walk out the bathroom door with the back of her dress tucked into her pantyhose for God and everyone to see. I, compassionately and quickly, stopped her and she thanked me profusely for saving her from a completely embarrassing experience. I have gratitude that I had compassion as opposed to carrying the energy of judgment, jealousy, anger, or contempt. It's a sad state to be in and expose others to and is a completely dysfunctional place to bond with others (judging others as a team sport, for instance).

Think about the past three times you judged anything or anyone (the tiniest situations). What did you gain and lose by creating this judgment? Think about the past three times you felt judged (don't analyze if you truly were, simply observe how you felt)? Imagine the judgment energy, you created and/or that you allowed yourself to be affected by, becoming a glass of water. Would you drink it? If you did, what would it taste like, what emotions would it conjure?

Goal Setting, Meditating and Meeting your Guides

"Our life is what our thoughts make it."
—*Marcus Aurelius, "Meditations"*

AFTER GIVING BIRTH TO MY third child, I had gotten away from my quiet time. My meditation time. The word meditation conjures up various visuals depending on the person. A chapter in my first book, *Adventures of a Mainstream Metaphysical Mom,* talked to the one-minute-meditation. There are books galore on taking you into deep or altered states but I simply wanted to integrate some type of meditation into my life that I could stick to with three kids, a full-time job and doing daily life.

My affirmation/goal was "I pay attention to my inner self at all times" so I put some timelines against this idea with meditation being one of the tools to accomplish "paying attention to me." In six months my vision was to meditate 15 minutes, three to four times per week and get to know my non-physical guides. By the twelfth month, I would find one or more teachers (physical or non-physical) to help me reach all realms (guides, angels, physical, etc) with ease (like turning a light switch on and off). This ultimately gave me access to universal wisdom (found in myself) to live a full and happy life in the physical and spiritual realms.

There are perceived prices to pay sometimes when we set goals and we, many times unknowingly, create blocks to keep from accomplishing them. When I looked at the six month goal, time away from family, work and sleep was a possibility but the fear that I simply would fail at accessing my guides was the biggest stumbling block. Twelve months down the road, I would take 100% responsibility with what happens in my physical and spiritual lives knowing that I had access to universal knowledge (lying within). This didn't mean that I could see "dead people" but more that I was expansive enough to feel my way to the truth of living happily—pretty beefy stuff for just doing a little bit of meditation or quiet time to gather my thoughts. But I promoted myself to truly living my vision and trusting my inner (intuitive) self without (or, at least, fewer) questions. This didn't mean that I got literal yes or no answers, but my physical and/or spiritual bodies would point in directions that would get me to my ultimate answer. I have complete access to all universal wisdom at the time that is right for me. The "time is right" is not necessarily your time clock but the Universal time clock and that takes perseverance and faith.

While re-writing this section of my book, I had an overwhelming urge to take a short nap. When I did, I dreamed that I was on my computer and downloaded a virus. Literally, a virtual bug was crawling across my screen and I had to answer a number of questions on the static screen involving "New Age" information to get my computer back to working order (at least that was the promise of this virus). While answering questions, in fear mode, I found a new idea that I felt would be very useful to the masses.

While I was excited about the new discovery, I worried about whether I backed up my hard drive (all other ideas and processes that move me forward). So even with the fear there was a place for discovery, excitement and new beginnings.

Owning your existing ideas about meditation and imagining new possibilities by allowing your mind to wander a bit is one of the keys to success. You'll develop your own opinions and preferences through life experience. Taking baby steps and establishing some type of deadlines knowing that some flexibility is built into them will give you a sense of accomplishment. So in six months I may celebrate my physical and non-physical relationships getting me closer to my ultimate goal. And in twelve months, I may celebrate the empowerment of choice and the lessons as a result of my relationships in all realities connected to these goals. Or maybe I celebrate accomplishing some pieces of the six or twelve month ideas.

Now this may seem a bit much but it became a real stumbling block for me so I really needed to figure out what was keeping me from achieving meditation regularly. When I had completed my 15 minute meditation action plan, it felt achievable and I found that I went deep quickly to test out my theory. Once I was in a relaxed state, I asked my guides, angels, higher self to assist me on my left and right sides (as if supporting me while walking). I imagined them holding my arms on both sides as I began my turbo trip. When I made up my mind that I was going to do 15-minute meditations three to four days a week, this etheric support gave me a sense of safety from committing any metaphysical faux pas while in an altered state. You can pretty much figure that, although you intend to do one thing, you'll probably do something very different, but there seems to be comfort in knowing that you think you know. Interestingly enough, since I set this fifteen minute goal, I make it back to physical reality within the set timeframe (almost like how we automatically wake up at a certain time in the morning).

Sometimes it slows people down to think about meeting guides, higher selves, divine entities, creating and seeing sacred places. Some would say so intimidating that they gave up on the process. If this is an issue for you, in your mind's eye (not in meditation) think about entities that have intrigued you in the past. Are they angels, faeries, God, Jesus, Buddha, Druid priests and priestesses, ancient beings, dolphins, unicorns, other mythical creatures? Write that down on a piece of paper. Then think about all the elements that lift your spirit. Are they crystals, waterfalls, ancient trees, beaches, oceans or other bodies of water, open fields of grass, ancient stones (Stonehenge for instance), ancient castles, roman pillars, islands with palm trees? Jot down this information. Build a virtual sacred space complete with entities and then visit it in meditation and see what develops.

Integrity and the "Me, Me, Me" Thing

"This above all: to thine own self be true, / And it must follow, as the night the day, / Thou canst not then be false to any man.
                                        —*Shakespeare, "Hamlet" (1600)*

WINTER, REGARDLESS OF what "faith" you embrace, can really be a challenge. For those in the United States, October through December is a major holiday hooplah… Halloween, Thanksgiving, Chanukah, Christmas, Kwanzaa… It's a buying, giving, receiving frenzy and no matter how much money you have it never seems to be enough during this time of the year. Emotions range from joy, happiness and excitement to victim, martyr, and anger resulting in depression. Dysfunctional behaviors that accompany these emotions are accelerated from the highest to the lowest levels.

I'm acquainted with a woman who married a widower and co-parented his biological children to adulthood. In essence, she was their true mother figure as they lost their biological mom early in their adolescent development. Her step-children, now adults with their own children, always asked for very expensive gifts... refrigerators, expensive clothes, high-end electronics... and she felt obligated to purchase them. However, when she did purchase these expensive items she resented it. She and her husband established a budget for the holidays every year but she never stuck to it as she allowed her children to manipulate her. After the third year of hearing her complain about this situation I blurted out (oops), "Your affirmation should be, I am a loving mother with clear boundaries." They obviously knew who to manipulate to get their ways since childhood and it was way past due to realize that love wasn't attached to her pocketbook. Her choice to allow the manipulation was making her miserable. She knew she had to put her foot down and took baby steps to push this manipulation out of her life from the twenty dollar requests ("Mom, can you pick me up a present for... I didn't have a chance to.") to clearly stating, "I'm sorry but I simply can't afford to buy you a refrigerator." It didn't make her manipulative step-children happy, but it sure gave her peace of mind and that's what this was about.

Owning a business for seven years (as I write), people come and people go. Situations change and sometimes events can be handled with grace and other times not. A talent within my company decided to go in a direction that created some strain on our business relationship (and somewhat personal as a result). While I understood this move as a friend, I quietly wondered how this was going to affect my overall business. With no new products from this partner for nearly two years, the product sales began to drop and I had to make some decisions on whether to manufacture more. Thinking much too much, I began to analyze how this person changed direction without regard to my welfare, how his actions communicated that he only cared for what was best for him. If I hadn't made a number of changes in my business before he went off half cocked, I would be out of business...!

But wait a minute! Flip side. If he can't pay bills, what decisions does he have to make to take care of himself? If he's struggling to attain the basics, can he take others' feelings, welfare, situations into account? So Me, Me, Me is about survival with the vision of achieving happiness over time. But let's not forget that an important ingredient to "Me Me Me" is integrity.

As a mother of three, if food, shelter, clothing, marriage, and health aren't at risk, I can sprinkle on some courtesies to others. It may not make me the most popular person in the world as I express my boundaries but I do this with integrity. It's been my experience that when I hear, "No matter what... I will never... Always... All the time..." I know that the Universe is giving me the warning signal that it will "No matter what, always, all the time CHANGE." So if you hold the vision of being a (wo)man of your word, be careful what operative words you use. If you don't see people respecting your boundaries, ask yourself, "What words or non-verbal cues am I communicating that create that situation?" Be honest with yourself and others when you take care of you and understand when others are doing the same.

Wanting and Needing and How it Can Create Chaos in Your Life

"Want is a growing giant whom the coat of Have was never large enough to cover." —Emerson, *"Wealth, The Conduct of Life"* (1860)

LARRY HAD CONSISTENT personality clashes with the owner of a company that he was financially very successful with for about two years (even making salesperson of the year). Reaching his limit on the conflicts on the job, he made a move to a competitor. He had a non-compete clause with the company he left and it ended in a very difficult lawsuit. For the next few years, Larry hopped from job to job because of perceived larger money-making opportunities. In addition, he worked on a network marketing concept part-time to try and build that business. All the while he complained that he really didn't like what he was doing and looked forward to the time that he was talking in front of hundreds of people to help them improve their lives. However, Larry didn't know what he was going to teach, he only "knew" that people would be listening.

His wife, home full-time to care for their two small children in addition to caring for her middle schooler from her first marriage, was thankful that she was home raising her children. It was tight, but she cut lots of corners, and was doing some home parties for some extra cash.

Larry made sure that his home followed all the feng shui rules (as well as integrated additional practices) for success with his primary intention of making a whole lot of money. He was confused, however, that within a three year time-frame, they had to file bankruptcy. Coincidentally (maybe, maybe not), there was a haunting symbol directly next door as their neighbors filed bankruptcy, left their cars in the driveway, home vacant, and ended their marriage. The house next door was still vacant (for nearly two years) when Larry and his wife filed bankruptcy.

In frustration, Larry exclaimed, "I'm doing everything I'm supposed to do for feng shui to manifest money. Plus, I'm saying affirmations constantly! What am I doing wrong?" While symbols and processes are powerful, they can also be tricky if you are being exposed to contradictions. While I am very conscious of feng shui, other symbols and practices, it is extremely important to establish clear, realistic goals, live them consistently, with grounded affirmations that truly make your mark.

A friend asked Larry after hearing him say many times, "Some day I'm going to be talking to hundreds of people about something and they are really going to listen." The question in return was, "Why do you want people to listen? What healing message do you have? How can you help others?" His response, "I don't know yet." His constant search for something better became very intense and his health began to reflect this. His work record became complicated, and it was difficult to explain why he switched jobs so much. Even though Larry was over-qualified for some job opportunities, the better companies could no longer consider him because he became a risk rather than a reliable asset. His financial, intellectual, physical, social and spiritual matters needed some serious analysis and prioritizing with clear timelines so that he could tackle one goal at a time.

Since he and his wife filed for bankruptcy, the first priority was to get their financial matters in order which would include stabilizing his career. He was heard on a number of occasions saying, "I need more money." This affirmation puts him in the "need" mode as opposed to, "I am achieving prosperity." There weren't any solid actionable steps, he was simply needing and wanting and the energy in these words encouraged him to move from one opportunity to another so he stopped using these words.

Now Larry states that "I am successful in all that I do." In bankruptcy, he stuck with a job to clean up his record, he learned to actually like his job, and stabilized his income.

His next area of life could include his intellectual and spiritual development given all his life lessons. He is obviously on the road to achieving his dreams. His success story may become a book(s) and workshops. He has more gratitude for what he has this very minute: three healthy children, a solid marriage, a nice home, and a stable income. He is thrilled that, even though money is tight, his wife can stay home and care for their young children.

There isn't an end to the story, there are simply constant beginnings. Larry and his wife have definitely had some serious financial, intellectual, physical, social and spiritual lessons. How do your hard luck stories play out? Who's to blame for your issues (lost my job, bad market conditions, bad teacher, someone or something else caused your problems)? After you write your stories, take a closer look at who you are blaming for your misfortunes to create an internal awareness then say "It's over, I have to move on to improve my quality of life." The lawsuit against Larry began his downward spiral, but moving on is imperative for his expansion. You can't control others actions (no matter how hard you try), but you can decide on the approach to take to heal.

The Perfect Plan for the Perfect Job

"The mind covers more ground than the heart but goes less far."
—*Chinese Proverb*

HELEN WAS NEWLY DIVORCED from her husband of nearly ten years. Solo was a theme she was becoming very comfortable with and she decided to start her own sewing business. I met Helen at one of my goal setting workshops. We were going through some exercises and she said, "I'm trying to line up all my plans so if this doesn't work out, I can fall back on something else." Now I'm all for being realistic and have been known to advise people to transition into new businesses by holding down two jobs but responded (more intuitively), "How much time is 'Plan B' taking you and what about 'Plan A'?" I asked her about her cash reserves and what she had done to build and promote her new business. She had the right amount of money and the phone was ringing regularly so I suggested to put Plan B on hold and dive into Plan A and "Pretend like there is no other plan so that you can focus on the success of your new venture."

Well, word traveled fast on the quality that she put out and within, literally, three months, she had hired three other reliable women to sew for her and had to turn down business (even an offer to do about two-hundred thousand dollars per year as a back-up sewing room). Helen took the complete leap but did it because it's what she loved to do, create through sewing. No matter what, she knew that she would have fun doing it. But she had a child to support and a house payment to make so being realistic was important, so second, Helen had some cash reserves and knew how long she could enjoy "Plan A" before she needed to consider other options.

Jane, another entrepreneur, was in sales (working out of her home) for an established mainstream finance management company that valued her as an employee. She, however, was looking to break into the body, mind, spirit industry as a consultant and product distributor. She mapped out her plan, ranked her tasks, gave herself deadlines and was feeling ready to take the leap. She was single with no children, her house and car were paid off and as we discussed her options she said with excitement, "I'm ready to do what I love so I'm going down to part-time with my mainstream job and develop my new business!" I responded, "Great, but why do you need to decrease hours of what is already a very flexible situation? You will do most of your consultations and classes on the weekends and after regular business hours. Since you don't have anything or anyone to tie you down, why not fill up your "free time" for the next six months to realize the potential?" There was no reason for Jane to drain her savings and put herself in a tight financial situation. Her current company regularly demonstrated its appreciation, and she was in the sales field so corporate wasn't breathing down her neck and her manager didn't micro manage her because she did a great job—perfect for an entrepreneur to do what she loved and still bring in the cash that she was accustomed to.

Even though Jane had the cash resources to go part-time pay, the income potential for the first (at least) two years would be disappointing to her in her new field. She had little experience in the new industry but would eventually find her "point of difference" once she gained enough experience in her spiritual endeavors. She was clever, extremely bright and aggressive while being pure of heart and intention so it was only a matter of time. But the time-line was years not months away.

There is no straight-forward right or wrong answer. Jane could have gone full-time into her new spirit-driven business and pulled from savings or part-time corporate America income and part-time new business. Unfortunately, she dropped her mainstream job entirely. Her learning was invaluable but not gentle as it turned out that she had some health issues within a short time-frame and dropped her health insurance. She became financially strapped which forced her back in the mainstream. Helen could have completely mapped out Plan B to give herself even more peace of mind but the affirmation that could crumble her ultimate goal would be, "There's always 'Plan B.'" For Larry, he'd done many things the hard way but, as he cleared his mind and intentions, he was back to flying to heights of his choice. He finally stayed with a company long enough to regain his title as the division's highest performing salesperson!

All very different situations. No wrong answers. Many roads to get to your divine location. Can you find any common links to your life experiences and Jane's, Helen's or Larry's? Given your life experiences and observing each of theirs, how could you apply learning to help you move through your challenges more gracefully?

Manifesting in Increments… Acknowledging your power

"The sole advantage of power is that you can do more good."
—*Baltasar Gracian, "The Art of Worldly Wisdom" (1647)*

I FOUND A NEW LOVE. It took 40 years to get there but I am lovin' yoga. My goal is not to become a contortionist but merely focus on good form and overall health. My goal is also to grow into this discipline with my husband.

My in-laws were the first to experiment with this idea when they entered their sixties. My husband started reading up on it and decided he wanted to give yoga a try, but never took the next step (that's my job in the relationship). He talked about it for a year or so and I finally said, "Tomorrow we go to our first yoga class." We did it and loved it.

It seems that all I have to do is think of a goal and it materializes in, literally, days. There was a little nagging reality called money when attending yoga classes more than once a week. So I planted a thought, "It would be great to fit this in twice a week." But doing this twice a week could get pricey because I held the vision that my husband and I could expand at a similar pace (so sessions times two). This would take us into a $200 per month investment and we simply didn't have the extra money to do this. But the vision of taking an additional class became a reality when I got a blanket email from the yoga studio saying they would trade administrative work for free yoga sessions. Thrilled, I jumped on this opportunity. Manifestation!

Taking it a step farther, my husband was out of town during our regular class but I just couldn't miss my new found body and spirit connection. As I sat in the lobby waiting for my yoga class to convene, I reflected on how nice it would be to get private lessons (like my in-laws) to really get my form right. I looked down and saw $55 per hour for private lessons. My wallet began to groan so I put this down as a lofty goal for the future. But then the magic kicked in... I was the only one in class this particular night and got a private lesson for a price I could handle.

I boasted to my husband about my private session and how I had been able to manifest major magic in many areas, including this one. When I talked to my intuitive coach about this magic during my monthly individual session she said, "What do you think creates that magical manifestation talent that you seem to have perfected?" I said, "If the vision is for my overall good and brings harm to none, then it seems to become a physical 'okee dokee.'"

But as I pondered this farther, I surprised my seventy-plus-year-old coach as I expanded my thoughts, "...However, I don't believe that you have to be pure of heart to create universal expansion." For instance, if someone obtains a parcel of land due to greed and overindulgence, some people would say this is unfair or bad. It may seem unfair at the time, but what if something really wonderful happened to this land much later? You only see the bad, greed, lust but the process leads to ultimate (the label) good.

What about the Holocaust? With certainty, the many people that lost their lives, lost family, and lost all their possessions would see these events as completely evil and served no purpose other than to prove bad can overcome good.

Hitler was a terrible man but I look at all of the movies, the books, and the museums with physical proof of this atrocity and ask myself, because of all of the accurate historical documentation, will it keep these types of things from happening again? I know that my middle-schooler has read dozens of books since elementary school, watched many documentaries, and wrote (and is still writing) papers on these types of crimes to humanity. I celebrate that she has a great deal of compassion and a critical eye toward anyone or anything spitting in the face of humanity. I am convinced that our children will be even tougher on these matters not tolerating prejudice and inappropriate judgment.

I was listening to a radio show the other day and a woman came on the air saying that the United States should profile all Islamic followers (referring to terrorism brought to the United States from those following the Islamic faith on September 11, 2001). She said they should put "them" all in one area and monitor them to figure out which are traitors to the United States and which are not. The radio host asked her if she felt the United States was right to put the Japanese in camps in the

20th century (which meant also taking all of their personal belongings). This, approximately thirty-year-old, fear-based, uneducated woman said, "Yes." Our children are our future. Educate them. Demonstrate courage. Fill them with compassion.

How do you manifest the good for you and others? Acknowledge the power of your thoughts every time they show up so that you are clear of the magic within. How do you help fill all minds with compassion (children to adults)? How do you demonstrate courage? How do you help others effectively stand up to those who are not humane? How do you define "good" and "bad?" How can you train your mind to see the "good?" Who is labeling "good" and "bad" to keep you from seeing the "higher good?"

Conquering Insurmountable Money and Other Issues

"Money is power, freedom, a cushion, the root of all evil, the sum of blessings."
—*Carl Sandburg, "The People, Yes" (1936)*

I WAS SITTING ON AN airplane coming back from a trade show that was 20% down from last year and doing some fear associated with that and a financial blip came up on the screen on financial management. The woman said, "It's my opinion that you get a 15 year mortgage instead of a 30 year because..." Then I started thinking, I know that I'm going to have a house payment for this entire lifetime and I'm okay with it. I know that I will probably have a car payment for this lifetime and I'm okay with it. I don't consider it debt. I consider it my property (and it is insured for financial protection) and the bank is just part of that mix. But I was getting a bit too intimate with this banking process.

I got home from my selling trip with some comfort in knowing that my expenses were covered. My mind wandered... how would I pay off the business running debt? Opening my mail, I had a certified letter from a distributor that said that they could only pay me 25% of what they owe me, but only if I signed a paper that said I would accept this as payment in full. Their threat, "If you don't accept this, we will be filing bankruptcy" meant I wouldn't get any type of payment. I wondered why they didn't include the 25% check regardless of what I agreed to (after all, they owed it to me) with their cover letter and said, "This is what we can do even if you don't accept our terms because we want to do the right thing." So it made me wonder, "What would my debtors think if I said, "Sorry, 25% or nothing!" But what a relief it would be to only have one quarter of the debt owed!

Before I left for my trade show trip, I wrote out all the checks to pay our people and bills on time. While I had a book of many receivables, few were paying on time, so I was short to pay all of the bills for my company. Emotions poured into my consciousness... I was upset and frightened that I wouldn't be able to do business with integrity as a result of not paying what I borrowed, feeling like I was failing, upset with the possibility that my company partners wouldn't be able to count on me... I had to calm myself down so I sat with my favorite divination cards and asked, "Is everything going to be okay?" Of course, the answer was "yes." What other answer could there be?

Finally making it to bed, I laid there with my mind racing. I talked to my guides, my angels, God, anyone who would psychically listen and said I need your help! It was the first time in my life that I ever considered doing something drastic. And why? Money? My job? My career? Then in came visions of my toddler laughing and squealing as she approaches a play area and says "play mommy," giving me kisses with her mouth open, speaking gibberish while pretending to read a book. My pre-teen going through puberty, becoming a beautiful young woman, an accomplished musician, determined athlete and dedicated scholar. My boy... the dancer, dramatic, creative, and a lofty scholar. Did they care what kind of job or career I had? What did money really mean to them if they didn't have a mom?

I once worked for a candy company and the vice president of manufacturing told me how disappointed his son was when he found out his dad merely oversaw the process and didn't actually make the candy. The burdens of responsibility are what we make them. I put myself into panic mode because I wasn't living in the moment. I was hanging out in the future of "what ifs," forgetting one of my cardinal rules of "intuitively knowing that everything will be okay."

I invested and owed tens of thousands starting my company seven years prior. Being too much of a heroine and investing in multiple talents, I fronted funding for many people and products. My inventory raw cost was valued at about one-third of the total debt. A number of customers were having difficult times making ends meet so my company was getting paid late and sometimes not at all. On a personal level, the market conditions had decreased our investment portfolio by about half over the past several years. I had been saving for a family trip for nearly two years (which was quickly becoming the money that would help fund this book). We were saving money for our kids' college funds and for retirement. We paid cash for vitamins, car repairs, most clothing, and many home improvements. And we had a solid amount of equity in our house. It was time to manifest my new reality in chunks. A longer-term vision was key. There was no quick fix.

The reality was that my company was not worth the amount of debt. If my physical body were to stop, I had plenty of life insurance to cover the debt so no one would be burdened and I would have paid all off with integrity. My company was its own entity and should take care of itself but I wasn't sure how realistic this was anymore. The art was managing this so that I wasn't worried about it all the time and to not get so down in the dumps that I stopped saving for other things (college fund, retirement, modest vacations). It was time to put some of my more extravagant activities on hold for five to ten years to cut back and pay off the debt.

My husband and I were out on a walk one night when I mentioned the dreaded amount of debt and he carefully responded, "I thought the debt was about 15% lower when we talked six months ago." He was right. It was mounting and I continued to invest in new products that I was sure would pay out quickly when I should have been focusing on the debt. He asked me what we needed to do and the simple answer was cut back, stop investing in new ventures and getting stuck with so many interest payments. My credit rating was great and I was going to keep it that way. In addition, I was determined to pay off the debts as opposed to running away from them.

I did most of my regular business spending on one credit card so that I could monitor it. On the overall debt figure, I held the vision of a monthly payment that felt realistic and would pay down the debt in about four years. I knew that this wouldn't entirely put me at a zero balance but, at least, it would get me closer to my goal.

It's like when you clear clutter, decorate a room or garden, you start with the basics and then you add-on over time or clear clutter a piece at a time. It happens because you have patience. You persevere and manage the feeling of being overwhelmed as much as possible when it hits you. Remind yourself that you have a realistic vision and that the major requirement is to stick to the plan and regularly observe the exact progress you've made. Don't devastate yourself by looking up at how high the mountain is, look back and see how far you've climbed and pat yourself on the back.

You can manifest in the physical when you have a realistic visual and timeframe. Many fall down the mountain because they want the quick fix. Start with something small to build your manifestation confidence. It doesn't have to be about debt. It could be about a decrease in pant size, how far you can walk, run or ride in a set number of minutes, saving for a vacation. Hold visions that are realistic. Don't set yourself up to fail by lying to yourself.

Did my plan to decrease debt work? I held the vision to manifest realistic amounts of capital for monthly bills and debt. This meant that we, gently and with gratitude, checked with customers if we didn't receive their payments on time and we worked the phones to make sure customers had all the information that they needed to put in their next orders. I found my company slowly but surely working on a cash basis as opposed to credit. Clearly my company would continue to pay bills on time (keeping my personal credit rating intact) but there are no quick fixes. Yes, it was scary but it continues to manifest because the intention is to do business honorably. When I cut up my first company credit card at zero-balance you'd thought I'd won the Pulitzer.

Identify one goal, work toward it in pieces, be focused and reward the baby accomplishments that get you to your ultimate goal. Redirect your fear energy to ignite the fire of your universal power to create all good things in your life! If you are physically docile, can you exercise three times a week for fifteen minutes for the next thirty days? Can you cut out eating after 8:00 P.M. for thirty days? If you have issues with clutter, can you clean out one closet or clutter gathering area every week-end for a month? Change pattern(s) that don't serve your highest good, celebrate your accomplishment after thirty days.

The Fear of Loss… What does it do to your perspective?

"Fear is sharp-sighted, and can see things under ground, and much more in the skies."   —**Cervantes, "Don Quixote"** *(1605-1615)*

My husband and our oldest child went to get pizza and the other children were upstairs playing. But things got too quiet and I yelled upstairs, "Where's your sister?" The response, "Up here." I asked, "Where up there, can you see her?" The response, "No." I jumped out of my chair and said, "Look for her now!" And I started yelling our toddler's name hoping she would answer, but nothing. I looked at the back patio screen. It was closed but something didn't feel right. I ran outside, in the dark screaming her name at the top of my voice. Within minutes I felt sick to my stomach, felt light-headed and was sobbing as I realized that she was not in the house, yard, or within immediate sight. Helpless, I didn't know where else to look. I couldn't find her. I lost my baby! How could I have allowed this to happen? Where was she?

Hysterical, I headed for the telephone to dial 911, but two young neighbor girls showed up on our back patio with our two-year-old. "Mrs. Payton, we were walking down the street and we thought there was a big rock in the road. We got closer and it was your daughter running down the middle of the street. A car was headed right for her." With tears in my eyes, I thanked the girls for bringing her home and saving her from certain injury, if not death. The best I could figure is she heard me screaming for her and thought it was a game to run away from mommy who was certain to catch her at any time. I was confused on how I should respond now that she was back in my arms, with anger or happiness? A two-year-old doesn't connect with, "Don't you do that again!" She went out to play!

I had another sick feeling with one of my other children at about age three, eight years prior to this incident. He was in the yard with his sister and she came in the house minus her brother. I asked where her brother was and she said, "I don't know." I rushed outside only to find that he was no longer in the front yard. I was frantic, only to find him in the bathroom ten minutes later with his diaper off smearing his feces all over the wall. I never thought I'd be so relieved to clean (literally) crap off my walls.

So I asked myself, given the world of lessons that I have chosen to embrace, what was the lesson here? Should I sell my company and super glue myself to my children? Was this a major lesson in responsibility for my son (who was supposed to be playing with his sister?) and did it work? Was this additional confirmation that my daughter is protected by major angelic energy and a message in faith? Was it all of these? None of these? Is the lesson not to have the answer?

I recalled a dream I had the night before. I was running with a figure that represented my husband and baby (the same child was found running in the street). People were chasing us and we were running from place to place (particularly airports) hiding so that we could keep our baby. We got to a point that we couldn't hide because too many people knew who we were. I had an odd fear of loss for my youngest daughter when I woke up on that particular morning (although I didn't actually experience them taking her in my dream). As a result, throughout the waking day I wasn't feeling safe. Maybe this was the reason why I felt uneasy about the silence upstairs and reacted within minutes. The fact that "they" didn't take her in my dream and that she wasn't taken from me in the physical was significant as well.

What I know for certain is that I don't like feeling any of these emotions… extreme fear of loss, pain of fearing a loved one is in danger or hurt (or going to be), displaced anger toward my children, guilt of not paying attention to the well-being of my children. However, under this type of stress, I react very quickly. The goal of protecting what's important to me does serve a purpose (even if it shaves a few years off this physical life).

I had been accused earlier in the day by my husband and two older children that I over-reacted to simple situations. This was brought on when my (again) toddler was sitting on my husband's lap on a swing in the park. I saw her let go and I let out a shriek as she flew off of his lap onto the ground. My husband was peeved because I shrieked. My older kids said, "Mooooooommmmmm!" My toddler just looked up at me not knowing whether to laugh or cry. My husband said, "You are like the 'boy who cried wolf' and people are going to stop listening to you." My theory is, "Always listen to momma because the general theme of over-reaction is connected with your safety or a lesson to be learned (even if you don't like the way it's communicated)."

There was a day when the only loss I feared was for my vehicles, money, physical possessions, home, professional positions, my youth, my slim physique and so on. Now my life revolves around my family. I'm no martyr (I still love to take care of and do things for myself) but I realize that you're truly "living" when your consciousness expands past yourself. Past your stuff. Past your titles. I like myself a lot more because I have more depth as a person. So my fear of loss has helped me celebrate the over-reactor in me to protect those I love. I'm celebrating the non-physical things that make me happy and strive to keep them in my life for as long as possible.

Write a list of people that have helped you become the person that you love in yourself. How do these people help you expand past yourself? Are there people in your life that bring out the least in you and you like yourself less? When are you going to get rid of them? Celebrate your expansion!

Feeling Alien While Still Being a Part of Community

> *"Mankind has become so much one family that we cannot insure our own prosperity except by insuring that of everyone else. If you wish to be happy yourself, you must resign yourself to seeing others happy."*
> —*Bertrand Russell, "The Science to Save Us From Science,"*
> *The New York Times Magazine (March 19, 1950)*

IT WAS THE FIRST VIOLIN concert for my son during the holiday season (December) and he had to be there thirty minutes early to tune his instrument and get organized so I decided to stay and get front seats for our whole family. I watched as families in our community poured into the cafetorium (cafeteria by day with stage to serve as an auditorium) and some energy projected hassle and strain. Others celebrated this event as an extension of the holiday seasons which included special grooming and ceremonial clothing. Others walked around, as if at a party, to greet other relatives and parents.

This day, I felt alien, like I didn't fit in. So when one of the "party parents" came by to chat, I was at a bit of a loss for words. When coming to a close, it was abrupt and awkward (but also a relief). I created a reality for myself on that particular night that said, "You really don't have much in common with these people so why do the 'small talk' thing?" Making sure I put myself even farther outside, one father warmly smiled at my husband and greeted him but didn't have the same greeting for me. Men bond with sports, compatible job descriptions and grilling ribs talk (I know this), but this night of all nights, I was extremely sensitive to being "out of the loop."

As we went out for ice cream after my son's debut, I was agitated. I didn't share it with anyone, but I couldn't get this miniscule interaction out of my head. I rehearsed in my head our next chance meeting. Perhaps I'd say, "The rule is when you greet one spouse with a smile, you do the same for the other." Or maybe I would just force him to talk to me and say, "You seem a bit uncomfortable around me, is there something you want to get off your chest?" It worked! I successfully alienated myself! I wasted quality family time and really made sure that I sunk to the farthest depth of negativity. You are what you think.

Not taking anything personally and not making assumptions that everything is about me is truly a challenge some days. During this time period, I had been working long hours to get ready for a major event, was introducing a number of new products, and had been going to bed no later (or I should say earlier) than 1:00 A.M. Fitting in family and inner circle time and preparing for the holidays as well, my social skills definitely needed dusting off. So certainly I'd feel out of place, alien, out of sync, disoriented in a social community setting.

Then a conversation with a body, mind, spirit oriented friend came to mind. She said, "I no longer have any friends outside of the body, mind, spirit circle." I wondered to myself, "Is this where I want to go?

Do I hang out where it's safe? Do I shut out the mainstream as it relates to my inner circle?" Isn't this what many organized religions or radical ethnic support groups do? Isn't this one of the ways that prejudice and judgment percolate which can then result in anger, violence and even death and destruction?

So it goes back to celebrating my uniqueness and yours. I strive to love my alien self while not shutting out neighbors, parents, those outside of my "idea range" or ethnic background who are reaching out (or not) to me. Think of a time when you felt "alien." What types of emotions did it conjure? What action(s) did you take as a result? Think about someone that you designated as alien (dig as far back as childhood). How did this person react? How can you turn each of these scenarios around so that you don't create energy this unproductive?

Cutting and Pasting Our Way to "Answers"

"New opinions are always suspected, and usually opposed, without any reason but because they are not already common."
—John Locke, *"The Epistle Dedicatory, An Essay Concerning Human Understanding" (1690)*

How do we build community? Many build this around a house of worship and, as physical beings, we are deeply influenced by the written word (good and bad). I keep books (on tape and written) in my van that I intend to read or listen to and this particular book had been sitting in my van for more than a year. I'd read a page or so at a time but one Christmas Eve, while my husband was driving to and from Cleveland for our traditional celebration with his parents, I devoured most of the pages during the four-hour van trip. This small book talked about the "Hidden Stories of the Childhood of Jesus" (by Glenn Kimball). In the "Holy Bible's" New Testament, there are very few stories about Jesus (in relation to this huge document based on Christian beliefs). You hear about His conception, His birth, then His adulthood, His passing and His resurrection.

So it really captured my interest when I found new ideas about Jesus like: Jesus may have actually been born in a cave before entering the city of Bethlehem because Mary couldn't wait; Joseph's lineage was that of physical "kings" and his family was wealthy; Jesus foretold (as a child) his demise on the cross and his family was actually saved, during His childhood, from being robbed by the same men that would be to the right and left of him during his physical death on the cross; Jesus was an avid supporter of women (politically incorrect through the ages, but particularly then); numerous women traveled with Jesus as men did; Jesus' adult travels were largely funded by women (making many of the men they were married to a bit out of sorts); the many infant/childhood miracles not recorded (healing utilizing Jesus' water bathed in as an infant...) as well as more about his gifted mother Mary.

You can throw out many theories as to why His childhood stories were not included in scripture and aren't studied by those who base their faith on miracles as a result of Jesus' presence, but there are many reasons to take a look at stories about Jesus (in addition to other studies). He professed that He was the Son of God and that we are all God's children. This made sense to our personal household as we embrace the idea that we are all a piece of God capable of manifesting "Jesus-like," Buddha-like,"... realities. This is, by no means, a belief to force onto you, but I am in awe of the magic that He was a part of and crave to fully realize my "power" as Jesus and other prophets did.

I'm not a theology expert, but this continues to point to the idea there are no complete answers. In fact, we, as a nation, continue to find stories about Jesus and other information of "biblical" proportions (or whatever your text)—not to mention the "Dead Sea Scrolls," wars and fires that have destroyed many sacred documents, and more. So many are, in essence, followers of cut and paste documents or incomplete thoughts unless they are allowing their souls to embrace what makes sense to them in addition to the written word.

I was watching Sesame Street with my two-year-old one day, and a muppet came in with a message that said, "I can come." Of course, this was great news until the muppet realized he missed a word: "not." "I can NOT come" changed the message entirely and the mood of those expecting a certain attendance. Forgetting about interpretation from religion to religion, going from Greek or Hebrew text to English (two languages translated from the "Holy Bible"), the same phrase translated from two different languages compared side-to-side interpret the verse "I am that I am" as also "I am being" (Greek versus Hebrew). Just a word or two. That's all it takes to change (sometimes completely) a message.

So what is re-incarnation? This idea has been embraced by those following Buddhist ideas and belief systems outside of Christianity. Some would say that re-incarnation is, in fact, supported in the "Holy Bible" as well and specifically by Jesus. Technically (according to the Oxford American Dictionary published by Avon Books) it could be defined as "bringing back (a soul after death) into another body." Now define "body." You, again, have to decide what makes sense to you but I propose the idea that a variety of teachings can be embraced, is subject to interpretation, and are all compatible because there is no complete answer in the physical. It requires (inner as well as outer) research, reading, and listening to many teachers to get to your place of comfort or peace. There's a possibility that as soon as you find your space, it will change as you are forever a student and forever changing.

Does this mean you shouldn't be a member of your community church? It may mean that you become a member of many churches, temples, synagogues... as they get you closer to your truth. However, know that everyone is in the spiritual place that they need to be in at the time. We are forever students. Ask yourself, what have I studied for the "answers?" How do I intuitively revise some of these thoughts to fit my truth? Has this created an honest, loving, compassionate, non-judgmental me? If not, what else should I be doing to get to that level?

Following Messages as Clear as Mud

> *"It requires wisdom to understand wisdom; the music is nothing if the audience is deaf."*
>
> —*Walter Lippmann, "A Preface to Morals" (1929)*

AT STILL ANOTHER LEVEL, in my (roller coaster of a) dream I was in a friend's store and she was going through a lot of changes. She was a New Age focused retailer, but her store had many things that were mainstream due to local pressures. She was marking down the mainstream merchandise to try to get rid of it and was very frustrated (particularly chocolate gifty items... no clue why). When I asked her customers for feedback on the store the response was, "It looks just like all the others." My storeowner friend asked me for some advice, we discussed a few ideas, transitioned into talking about a fund-raising idea for an organization of which we were both members then I announced that it was time for me to head home.

I went out the back door and found myself lost. There were numerous doors in the back of this building and I entered the first one that would open. Upon entering I was unable to get back out and a door to a downward stair well opened while the upper stairwell disappeared (the way I wanted to go was numbered up to 32). Finding that I was on level 13, I yelled out, "I'm tired of just getting hints. I want to hear or see you. Give me a clear message that this is the way to go!" Then I heard, "Hello." I yelled, "That's not enough. Who are you?" He responded softly, "Ben" (coincidentally this is spelled out randomly on my van license plate in my physical reality). He was a young man with red festive clothes (looked to be about 10 years old) and was about a head shorter than me. Without fear, I walked down the stairwell that led to nothing but industrial, painted, cement block walls. Then I walked back up the stairs to the original level with clarity, and feeling safe, regarding my divine direction.

Excited, I walked out the door that I originally entered. I had to find my friend and tell her about Ben and more! As I rushed back, I ran into another angel (an adult male) and his name was Slate and still another angel but I didn't catch his name. I noticed in passing that my friend's husband was coming out of one of the doors and had met at least one of the angels as well. I found her back in the retail mall (her location in my dream) and with excitement I expanded on a fund-raiser idea for the association.

They (trade association) had a wonderful newsletter and she and other members have contributed numerous articles on business matters that are helpful and informative. So I said, "Wouldn't it be cool if they provided a business building resource booklet for the industry (first booklet being divided into thirds somehow… again no clue why)?" We hugged and then I jumped into my vehicle (with BEN on the license plate) and finally headed home (eight hours away in reality and my children were with me).

There were a number of additional messages that I gathered on the way home in dreamtime. But when nearing the end of the dream rollercoaster, I was very tired. I was questioning whether I truly received divine guidance. I was frustrated, hungry, and concerned that my baby (fifteen months at the time) was not going to get the (restricted diet) food she needed. I stopped in front of a bed and breakfast. It was a sort of retreat. A number of people were in the sitting area and very content. I began to cry when I went up to the counter and said, "Reservation for Payton?" They said, "Hi Michelle, we have your reservation right here. If you go down to the kitchen, we have all the supplies you need for the baby."

When I shared this story with the storeowner in my dream, she went on to tell me that (on her drive home from the trade show) her husband (who I saw briefly in my dream) had just talked about doing a booklet for the trade association and how the price should be divided into thirds: a third for the association; a third for the cost; and a third to writers contributing their time! That following year the trade association came up with a complete guide for independent storeowners (including a CD) sharing marketing ideas, contracts commonly used, and other tips on how others have successfully run their stores.

Dreams can be very difficult because they don't fit together like a movie and many of the events will never make sense. But the major messages came together. This publication was angelically driven and became a reality for this group in less than one year. The friend that I had a dream about making major changes ultimately closed her store to pursue other national opportunities.

It takes some faith to follow messages that are as clear as mud. When you truly begin trusting your intuition connected to dreamtime (as well as other techniques… turning cards, psychic visions, "feelings"), you will be amazed at how you can improve your life. There is an art of following your intuitive self and guidance from the divine and applying it to the mainstream. Some process suggestions would be:

1. Keeping certain details to yourself on where you get the information in the mainstream and positioning it as, "I have a gut feeling... I would like to test out a personal theory... It occurred to me that... What would you think if..."

2. Write down your dreams, feelings, and/or visions immediately. If a dream, possibly even before you get out of bed so you don't forget any of the details. Many times, information doesn't make sense until much later but can provide clarity once realized.

3. Follow the messages. That's why they are given to you.

How has trusting your intuitive self been key to improving your life?

What's Love Got to Do with It?

"Where there is love, there is no pain."   **—*Spanish proverb***

I was exiting our neighborhood post office parking lot. There is a designated one way in and one way out. The driver of a big white sports utility vehicle decided that this wasn't convenient for her and pulled in the exit. She proceeded to park in a handicapped spot (and there were plenty of other spots in the lot). Then a healthy, attractive, mid-thirties to well-kept forties, woman hopped out of her vehicle and into the post office. Now, I'm aware I'm making some judgments here but I definitely wasn't feeling the love in her life force as she headed to her emergency call in the post office. The point is we all have something in common with that woman at that particular, uncaring, unloving moment.

Ever cut anyone off in traffic? Given people special hand signals from your car? Ever bounced up and down in your seat and said a few choice words (or, at least, had some insulting thoughts) in your vehicle as someone drives just a bit slower (maybe even the speed limit) than you? Ever give people dirty looks or had nasty thoughts while they are trying to give the exact change to a cashier? Ever taken a look at someone's outfit, body build, hair style, finger nails, automobile and made a quick judgment? Ever had a salesperson call you on the phone and you're just plain old mean? Ever in your life? Of course you have. We all have but how do we feel when we complete the action? We can justify it all we want, but is it really the energy that we want to own?

I find e-mail and driving to be loveless in many ways. For email, it can be a one-sided or delayed conversation that can be insulting, easily misinterpreted, manipulative, and physically (virus hoaxes) and emotionally (communication gone bad) destructive. When driving, many people maneuver their vehicles in aggressive, negligent, uncaring ways. In both instances, people seem to feel that if they can't be seen or touched, being loveless is okay. Hitting that "send" button or pushing those pedals gives us an inappropriate way of venting or projecting anger and frustration. I am guilty of participating in this dysfunctional circle and recently taped a phrase on my vehicle rear view mirror and computer "Cause no pain." That's it! I'm disgusted with myself at times!

When you slip, and you will, you can take it karmically back! It doesn't mean that you have to go over to the person you just judged and say, "Gosh, I'm sorry, but I just judged your (what I believe to be tacky) outfit and that wasn't good for my karmic health." But what you could try is:

1. Surround your negative thought with a beautiful golden or white light (if you visualize another color that's okay).

2. Watch the light completely cover the negative thought and carry it to heaven (or wherever you see as being a sacred place). If it's on a person or thing, be sure to pull the judgment off the physical entity so that your negative psychic residue is cleared.

3. Then give yourself a love wash and watch (in your mind's eye) more light wash your whole body from the tip of your head to the tip of your fingertips and toes and, again, carry it to heaven (or wherever you see as being a sacred place). And as a gift, do the same for the person or thing.

Others might say that there are much quicker ways to let go. The fact that you know you're sorry and can let go of the judgment may be good enough. But if you get regularly strung out and you see a pattern(s) forming (when you get in traffic you freak out, or a line at the grocery puts you on the edge), ask yourself questions like:

1. What is the deeper reason for my negativity (i.e. Why can't I wait my turn? Why do I consider myself the fashion police? Why is road rage an outlet for me?).

2. Sarcasm and jokes at others' expense aren't part of happiness. How can I take steps to not put myself in a situation to create unhappiness for others which then creates unhappiness for me?

If you find yourself becoming impatient in a car, can you listen to books on tape to expand your mind, keep you busy and positive? When someone has on an outfit that you can't stop thinking about, can you acknowledge that there are different definitions of beauty for a variety of reasons or maybe he/she can't afford the most flattering clothes? For the next thirty days, catch yourself when you find yourself doing loveless things and make a quick acknowledgement that it wasn't a fair judgment. If your judgments result in physical exchanges, try to acknowledge your inappropriate thought in the physical (not to mention plain old apologizing) then clear out the negative energy utilizing light healing.

Finite Money, Infinite Opportunities

"A wise man will make more opportunities than he finds."
—*Francis Bacon, "Of Ceremonies and Respects," Essays (1625)*

MY HUSBAND AND I had our house up for sale and got into the discussion of how one friend sold her house in three days and another in two months and still another not for a year and the why's involved. Then my husband's theory came out, "Well, it goes to show you, my theory is right. We have a finite amount of gold with money to back it up and someone has to lose for someone to gain." A bit surprised, I said, "How can you say that? The Universe has infinite opportunities." And then the old light bulb went off. Yes. Money is a great way to exchange energy, but is it the only way? No!

We were past due on getting our family photos done and my neighbor happened to be a good photographer. He needed a standard computer presentation done and the right computer to accomplish this. This wasn't a professional service I offered through my company, but I had the expertise (and time) to create a standard computer presentation and showed him how to make changes for future presentations and my husband went to the store to help him purchase the best system to do a traveling presentation. So we traded our time making it a win:win. We got a beautiful family photo package (pictures taken in a local park was a great perk as well). He got a professionally done computer presentation, additional computer training and hardware consulting that would have cost him, at least, fifty dollars an hour by a professional computer consulting or graphics company.

One of my cooperative partners created blessed jewelry for resale purposes to our network of stores. She retained a Shaman to bless the bracelets but he would not accept money. With much prompting he accepted some of the products he blessed as gifts (which made the designer feel like the circle was completed). Native American Indians, as well as other cultures, had trading blankets. They traded until they were equally satisfied. We grew tomatoes in our garden, our neighbor grew cucumbers so we traded some fresh produce. As a mainstream side note, be aware of the Internal Revenue Service rules if you are doing business-to-business trading so that you can experience infinite opportunities while still fulfilling government obligations.

Pokeman® cards, Beanie Babies™, baseball cards, Marbles (the game), baked goods for non-profit fund-raising, time donated to generate funds for a particular cause, and more are successful using this premise. Some are acquired through money, some traded on value. Just for kicks and giggles, take the time to write down some of your talents for trade. It doesn't mean you have to put a shingle out on your house or build a website around it, but you will begin to see the infinite opportunities available in the Universe. Do you bake, cook, clean, baby sit, mow grass, dig holes, draw, do secretarial and/or administrative work, or various consulting? Think about it. Apply it to your everyday life and watch your infinite opportunities grow.

So back to our house and the reality of physical money being exchanged. We built a house (a life dream of my husband) and hadn't sold our existing one so we had two house payments for a time. Our realtor was sure our house would be sold in the three months allotted (what we wanted to hear) given the location, the price, and the good condition. We sold it once but it fell through and, although we had many prospects come through the house (fifty families) there were no offers. Fear set in, as we went from one affordable house payment and being financially secure to two houses and possibly not being able to pay for either one of them! What were we doing? How could we put ourselves in this position? We had to quickly get over this fear or we were going to make ourselves crazy and, for certain, manifest selling our house for a price that wouldn't serve us. We gathered our emotions (my husband and I) and said, "It will be tight but we'll be okay. We can write off part of the interest loss on our taxes (glass half full kind of thing)." We moved into our new house and made sure we enjoyed it and didn't imprint worry and disappointment onto our past or existing home so that the energy would remain positive. Then my husband made a breakthrough. He said, "I'm not going to worry about this. It's only money!" I have to tell you that this was a huge breakthrough for him because there was a time when we were both on the high paying mainstream job track and it really was only money because we had a whole lot of it. But for someone to see it for what it is (only money) and not have an abundance of it, that's when clarity is gained. After all, our desire is not for money, but for what money provides as a result of the money exchanging hands. I will be the first to say that money is a solid exchange but it isn't the only way to manifest your reality.

With this worry out of the way, we made two house payments for only two months. Owners of another house in our area had it on the market for more than a year. They finally moved into their newly built home and rented out their other home. There are many ways to experience infinite opportunities. Make your list and expand out of the traditional box.

Loose Lips Sink Ships... Chit chat & gossip

"The best loved man or maid in town would perish with anguish/
Could they hear all that their friends say in the course of the day."
—*John Hay, "Distichs" (c. 1871)*

I ONCE WORKED WITH someone that could not stop bad mouthing others. She would visit accounts and make sure they knew how much she was being crapped on by other customers, other sales representatives, and other companies that she represented. When she was at trade shows, she would get into screaming matches with people she had past business dealings with and to make matters worse she had a real potty mouth. There was no "turning the other cheek" for this woman. One day she asked my opinion about her "situation." She asked, "Michelle, do you understand where I'm coming from?" My response..., "I understand there are patterns that you are repeating."

She was victimized at points in her life (join the rest of the world) and kept repeating this pattern. She was paranoid that everyone was out to get her, attempted to pull others into her world and sometimes it worked.

There are many reasons that people get loose lips: some are paranoid, some can't overcome jealousy, some are simply liars, some are looking to protect their interests (this could be for honest or dishonest reasons), some are looking for an artificial inner circle team to protect their backs (similar to all the reality shows that show people building teams).

Like most gossiping quarterbacks, they look for a team of heavy hitters to protect them. But the best functional quarterback is like the college football quaterback (2001) who won the Heisman trophy. He was known for going for the touchdown when his teammates weren't able to get to the ball in time, took the hits like everyone else, and won the respect of all his team mates as a result. He won respect by example, not with gossip and lack of integrety.

When I was commissioned to write for one of the premier New Age trade magazines, I was very proud and excited (a goal that I had set a couple of years prior). Not only do I get to write for an international magazine that I respect, I also got paid for it!!! Bonus!!! Upon my commission, I shared my good fortune with other members of my company. As much as they wanted to be happy for me, some were more concerned about my ability to effectively take care of their businesses. Fear is always rearing its ugly head so I had to remind myself that this was about their insecurities and not about jealousy, slighting my happiness, notoriety or success. I was in a particularly good space when this fear factor came up (it didn't emotionally phase me and I continued to do what was best for me), but sometimes it isn't possible to be objective, especially if chit chat rears its ugly head.

It was time to focus on myself too, with no guilt. This not only meant my writing career but just plain old me. From my perspective, it wasn't an either/or. If it was I would no longer have business or any other partners, because when you combine energy it is supposed to be a win: win. My youngest was two years old and my oldest was twelve, and I was ready to re-introduce myself to massages, spontaneous romance with my husband, lunches with friends, catching a movie and getting a coffee or hot chocolate afterwards, sitting next to a fire reading a book or paper... you get my drift.

So when chit chat and gossip is aimed at you, ask yourself, does it really matter what "they" think? If it doesn't, then stay your course. If it does, ask why does it matter? Is it personal or simply a projection of others' insecurities? If you're going to change your life direction because of chit chat, then get as close to the truth as possible. Upon evaluating it, would you find that certain people simply shouldn't be a part of your life in order for you to make progress?

"Let us live while we live."

—Phillip Doddridge, Quoted in
"Job Orton's Life of Doddridge" (1764)

Increasing Quality of Life when Chaos is On the Rise

"The tranquility or agitation of our temper does not depend so much
on the big things which happen to us in life, as on the pleasant or un-
pleasant arrangements of the little things which happen daily."

—La Rochefoucauld, "Maxims" (1665)

SOME THINK THAT IT MEANS YOU AREN'T really working when you have an office out of your home but I have been doing this for nearly 7 years (as I write) and co-raising 3 children. My toughest challenge came with coodinating getting pregnant with our third child, growing my business to international status, growing our new and existing lines, writing my books, and promoting my personal work. I continually reminded myself of how wonderful my life was but I could get downright grumpy and my oldest (11 at the time) sat down to dinner with the family one night and told me so. She said, "Mom, I really like you being home when we get on and off the bus and when Daddy's out of town, but you seem to get mad easier when we get home from school and you work a lot more." I asked her when she felt this began. Was it lately, last year, two years ago, from the beginning? We narrowed it down to when I became pregnant with her little sister. I was tired a lot and once the baby was born I had to tend to the baby during the day (nursing, changing diapers, sometimes napping to catch up on my sleep) and a lot of my work had to be done at night to play catch up.

One of the reasons why my husband and I decided to build a house was so we both would have home offices. My office was in a loft with no walls. I could hear everything going on in the house and vice versa. My business line also rang through the entire house so everybody in the household lived and breathed The Left Side. This all changed when we moved into our newly built house. Our business phone lines were wired separately so that we could unplug our phones at night and our fax lines were behind closed doors (no more fax rings echoed through the house). In addition, we added insulation to my and my husband's office walls so that the kids could get more rowdy when they got home. I also decided that I was going to subcontract additional work so I could free up more personal time and increase our quality of life.

So my job was to have more fun and be happier. However, on certain days the happiness meter ran out. It was 11:30 A.M. on my number 3 child's first birthday. My husband had been out of town for 4 days and I was operating on minimal sleep. My 11-year-old called from school to tell me that she forgot her violin and needed it by 1:00 P.M. I had a physical work-out scheduled for 12:30. My toddler needed to eat her lunch. I was printing information that had to get to the post office yesterday. The phone was ringing. I was hungry. And I was having a little birthday party for the baby. Repeat after me, *I am peaceful and calm,* **I am peaceful and calm,** **I am peaceful and calm.** What kept me from losing my head (entirely)? How did I find the happiness? Through gratitude.

Another more mainstream phrase would be "looking on the bright side." I had gratitude that my schedule was flexible and I could leave work and drop off my daughter's violin, go to and pay for my work-out, have a variety of quality food in the fridge to grab a healthy light lunch, and, bonus, my mother was in town, so she fed the baby while I went to my work-out. Thank you Universe.

These are not huge problems but they add up into one clump of chaos and can create discontent. Sometimes it gets so deep that you don't know where it began and how to find the end. This can tie your physical and spiritual bodies up in knots and sometimes we make decisions that make the situation more serious than necessary. And the simple things are what most chaos is wrapped around (no sleep, too many things on the family and/or business calendar, etc.). The key to preserving healthy, happy brain cells was appreciating the blessings at the moment of discontentment as well and understanding that situations flow a particular way due to the choices that I've made up to that particular point. I may still have stress but it will be minimized and, many times, unimportant at the end of the day (unless I've over-reacted and created a negative situation). To get to gratitude, sometimes I have to acknowledge that something terrible has happened but here are the good things to come, growth and lessons learned.

Start small with this concept. Death, loss, despair are usually too emotionally charged to get to a place of happiness without practice. We have so much stuff coming at us, there are many things to turn around daily. If someone purposefully cuts you off in traffic, you may have gratitude that you're not in that type of negative space because your life is so full. If you lost a personal belonging, maybe the person finding it truly needs the item more than you. If you miss an appointment or meeting due to traffic, maybe you weren't supposed to be there. Practice on the small irritants starting today.

Why We Get Permission to Give Advice

"There is nothing which we receive with so much reluctance as advice."
—*John Addison, "The Spectator" (1711-1712)*

SOMETIMES I CAN GET so caught up in how clever I am, I forget to ask permission before giving "advice." I was fortunate to find a teacher in an area that required quality mainstream training in marketing. He was very accomplished and I was aware of the divine intervention that brought him into my learning circle. I noticed after our training sessions were over, he would keep me for a while to discuss some of his personal processing which resulted in my feeling a bit soul-connected with him as well. Part way through our training, he had a terrible accident and I, with my infinite spiritual wisdom and resources, diligently thumbed through one of my handbooks. I described what area of the body symbolizes what issue and provided a rundown of new spiritual thought to move past the pain. My additional commentary included how this accident was a message for him to change his life and congratulated him on his rebirth.

Well I can tell you that this letter changed my life. I was fortunate that this teacher called to blast me! There were many lessons learned in that thirty-minute listening session that included a slew of four-letter words coming at me. Two of my lessons were: Even if the information was true, it couldn't have come at a worse time; and (although I thought I was a teaching resource to him as well) he didn't ask for feedback on why he was put through all that pain and was insulted as well as angry.

My husband happened to be home at the time and observed the one-sided phone conversation and when I hung up the phone he said, "What was that all about?" After giving him the shortened version of my message then his response, trying to put myself in the angry former-teacher's position, I told my husband, "Now that I'm back to my original weight after having our last baby, let's say you made a comment like, 'You were really heavy with your last pregnancy but now you look great!' I may or may not like the comment but that's better timing than if I were pregnant and you said, 'Honey, you've really gained a lot of weight with this pregnancy, but I know you'll get rid of the weight once the baby is born.' It doesn't matter if it's true or not."

But even though my words created emotional rage for this individual, I couldn't apologize for the information that I gave him. I could only thank him (and his inner circle) for being life teachers. In order to grow I have to be okay with that, living the idea that everything happens for a reason. Only those who try, make mistakes. It's part of the process.

One day I was at a company picnic (in my twenty's at the time) and I was talking, as usual. An employee's spouse, who elected himself my advisor that day, said, "I don't think you want to say that... Do you really think that's appropriate?" I was embarrassed and annoyed at the same time. I wasn't looking for advice and I was insulted. From that point on, I avoided this guy like the plague. Some things are best left unsaid unless you are asked for the information or considered a teaching resource.

He lived with the consequences of giving feedback that was considered criticism, judgment and sarcasm as opposed to advice. I lived with the consequences of this former teacher thinking I was a New Age crazy that didn't have a grip on reality.

The next time you feel like you want to give advice unsolicited, ask yourself: Does this person or group view me as a teaching resource? Is my opinion truly going to heal the situation or is keeping my mouth shut until I'm asked for my opinion (or given an opportunity to smoothly transition my thoughts) a better strategy? Why do I feel the need to give my opinion?

Seeing Past the Delivery

"Without feelings of respect, what is there to distinguish men from beasts?"
—*Confucius, "Analects" (6th C. B.C.)*

WHEN IN VARIOUS GROUP settings, people share opinions and exchange ideas. Each participant has to decide if he/she can be responsible enough to listen to a rough delivery to get the most complete information or take the easy way out and allow the smoothest delivery to influence him/her. I'm not saying that good delivery begets bad information; I am merely saying that usually the person with the smoothest delivery "wins" regardless of the reliability of the information. I had a mainstream manager who was a wonderful presenter even when the information that he presented was complete crap. But because of this beautiful delivery, he was rarely questioned on content. In fact, he is the president of a large international company today! He is very accomplished and has seen the error of his ways (in my humble opinion) but there were times where it was obvious that he simply did not respect his audience enough to tell the complete truth so that he could get his way. When people own these types of behaviors, it also reveals the disrespect that they have for themselves.

No doubt, listening can become very difficult when a person doesn't have some type of style. In the media, charm is everything (doesn't make it right, but it is what it is). However, if you are a completely effective leader (defined in more ways than one) and are working toward balancing yourself in body, mind and spirit, then seeing past the delivery to the truth is crucial and results in overall growth of the listeners and the presenters.

When working for a large packaged goods company, I was in a meeting when a question was asked of a line supervisor. She knew the information better than anyone in the room, but spent so much time worrying about delivery that she couldn't get it out effectively. The president (whom I enjoyed immensely as a person as much as a leader) basically said, "Could you give that information to me differently? I'll listen regardless of your delivery." There were people in the room pooh poohing her delivery, but those interested in treating others with respect (regardless of title) learned the truth by listening closely and deciphering accurate information. Some situations require savvy, but think of the honest information you are rewarded with when patient.

Another experience in corporate America when creating new products and campaigns revealed that politics were thick at times and we (marketing) had become a bit big for our britches and decided that sales representatives should have a scripted presentation in order to succeed with our new product introductions. Sales representatives that had been with the company for decades were dealing with the disrespect that comes with the "Adminisphere": decisions that are made by organizational layers above you that are often inappropriate to the problems they are designed to solve. A sales representative, and extremely kind soul, that followed a slower paced lifestyle which included his speaking patterns, was required to use the scripted presentation from corporate. His manager accompanied him and insisted he follow it verbatim (so as, according to management, not to lose the opportunity). This took some time and his manager began to fidget and said (in front of the buyer), "We should speed this up so we're not wasting 'Mr. Buyers' valuable time." The respectful buyer said, "Don't worry about it, you just take your time." Chalk one up for the buyer and his valuable time! The listeners and the presenter grew immensely that day.

When you're in a group setting and you speak, when do you feel respected? How do you feel when you are telling the truth? How can you make others feel respected and hold the vision of telling the truth? How do you feel when others react to your being a respectful, detailed listener (verbally or non-verbally)? Do you fall for the charmers or do you look for content to make the best decisions?

Can You Really Look Good at Others' Expense?

"Prejudice. n. A vagrant opinion without visible means of support."
—*Ambrose Bierce, "The Devil's Dictionary" (1881-1911)*

IT WAS EARLY IN MY marketing career and I was getting a big taste of how a few corporate Americans tried to rise to the top. I was in a meeting with our advertising agency and did not feel comfortable in a number of the energy fields I came in contact with. One, in particular, was set on making sure I knew "my place" during this particular brand (product) strategy meeting. He didn't much like when I gave feedback (after all, what value could I add being so "junior") but I figured I was the client and if my boss didn't want me in the meeting, I wouldn't have been there. It was my ordained day as this ivory tower account executive had taken a bit too many shots over time and decided to flash a few of his credentials at this meeting (commonplace in this setting). He went on to talk about his many years of experience with feminine hygiene products with one of the top packaged goods companies in the world, looked over at me and said, "Michelle, you are too young to know about this product…" I interrupted him and said, "If it's one thing I have a bit of experience in, it's feminine hygiene products. I'm sure I'll be able to keep up." There was a moment of silence in the predominantly male conference room. And, for once, he was at a loss for words.

Even common social or family settings can become blood baths when the "harmless" jokes or "put downs" start to spread like a virus, using victims like blondes, women, men, and ethnic groups. My kids have been known to tell "blond" jokes and I simply refuse to listen to them. Insulting and stereotyping someone else for a laugh or for betterment of one's status is an artificial, temporary fix to deeper insecurities.

When I was in my early teens, my mother had a few friends over to socialize. There was one particular guy that I could not stand being in the same room with. It's important to know that he was in his cowboy hat and (wearing a whole lot of) turquoise at the time. As he entered our living room, I leaped to the nearest exit but as I passed him I heard him say, "There's nothin' worse than a (certain ethnic group) wearing a cowboy hat." Well, that was it for me and I turned around and said to him, "Tom (fictitious), I wasn't aware that you were much of a cow puncher to earn the honor of wearing that hat!" All my mother's friends eyes were on me with mouths wide-open and Tom responded, "Shut-up,

Michelle!" And I in turn responded in my annoying teen-age, know-it-all tone, "You shut-up!" The last time I bumped into this guy, he was doing the Renaissance Festival circuit attempting to speak old English when he was still challenged with mastering his native English tongue (is "ain't thou" a phrase?).

Unfortunately there are folks out there who put others down to feel like they are ahead (and sometimes they succeed). If you are the victim of this type of behavior, there aren't always golden opportunities to protect yourself gracefully and when frustrated by this you may make yourself look bad. Ask yourself, what is the price you will pay for attempting to lash out to even the score? If you are the victimizer, ask yourself why do I need to hurt others to move ahead?

Too Many Deadlines… Crisis management to keep your head from exploding

"You ride astride the imaginary in order to hunt down the real."
—*Breyten Breytenbach, "Return to Paradise" (1993)*

OUR HOME WAS UP FOR SALE and we were building a new house. My company's biggest trade show of the year was coming up in less than two weeks. After two months, no offers were in-hand on our existing house and our neighbor's house sold within a week of putting it on the market. Our new house builder announced that we needed to close one day after I got back from my big trade show. It was the last week of school and many parties, final tests and gifts for teachers were also all on the list of things to do. My cooperative partners (artists/designers) were all behind in getting information I needed to prepare price lists, update the website and company literature. Daily "stuff" had to be taken care of (my toddler's needs, dinner, wholesale orders, production...). My company was introducing numerous new products at the trade show including my first book! Even as I was writing this section in my book, I could hear my baby playing in her bed and hoped she wouldn't cry so I could finish putting some thoughts to paper.

I was at my wits end and my brain truly could not handle one more detail but everything still needed to be done at the same time. I needed help to sort out the frustration, stress, worry, helplessness, anger, remorse, confusion, and fatigue in five minutes or less. My vibration hit a major low. How could I handle this all with grace so that I didn't look like a total bitch by the time it all passed?

We all go through these periods and sometimes we can't handle it all with grace. Everything happens for a reason and at its own time. I would just have to be okay with the flow of the universal time clock. So I broke the chaos up into little chunks to cope with the pressure.

• If we didn't actually get to take possession of the new home that we built with such love and care, then we must have built the house for someone else, right? I tried to give myself that little pep talk but with those lines came a great deal of remorse. I couldn't bring myself to even visit the new (nearly completed) home since we hadn't received an offer on our existing home. Maybe if I detached it wouldn't hurt as badly?

• If my (first) book wasn't delivered on time for the trade show, then it wasn't supposed to happen and I would introduce the book next year. Was my lesson in patience or was this the Universe's way of introducing my work at a better time?

• If my partners didn't give me information in time, then we wouldn't introduce their new items at the big show. Should I have been working with these new items if it was going to be too stressful? Was the Universe saving me time and money by making it so challenging that I wouldn't introduce certain new products?

• If I was a good mother, shouldn't I have been focusing on my children's last week of school, parties and teachers' gifts? Shouldn't I have taken my toddler out for more walks every day to enjoy the warmer weather? Was I missing out on life?

Obviously, I was stressed and questioning every possible life decision. Unfortunately, when we are in these types of situations, we have to ride it for a time because that is life. The question I had to answer for myself after hitting my low point, was how could I get back up? On one hand, I wanted nothing more than to go to my local psychic so he could tell me, "this is what's going to happen with your book; these new products will do well for you and these you will lose money on (so don't do them); you're going to get an offer on your house on "x" day and it will be for the amount that you will be happy with; your husband and kids love you, warts and all!"

It was more work, but I took a more empowered way out. When I talked to my intuitive coach I said, "It's time to feel better and get some of this chaos off my plate." She responded, "What if I hold the thought that your existing home will sell for the price right for you so that you are able to move into your new home without worry?... When you begin to worry, let it go and let someone else hold it for you." I was out on a mental limb so I tried it. And moved onto my next stress points.

I told my husband that I could keep the house straightened for potential buyers of our existing home (with a little help from my older children). He would deal with the last detailed decisions for both new and existing houses and the loans associated with buying and selling of each. Distancing myself from the planning process distanced me from the stress. Keeping the house clean was more in the moment and a more comfortable place for me.

Then I worked on getting ready for the trade show, a very rigid, inflexible deadline so I had to prioritize "must haves." I processed daily orders immediately (big priority since I don't get paid otherwise). I let go of the regret associated with deadlines not being met. As I let go, my book was delivered ten days earlier than the printer committed to. Loan issues to own two houses were resolved (by my husband). Five days after my intuitive coach and two other inner circle friends held the vision of our house selling for the price right for us, we received a satisfactory offer and sold it. A little perk... my husband's company even gave him some additional stock options at the end of this hectic week. I moved past the things that didn't come through and celebrated what did.

Not a day after I got my vibrational footing back, a friend called with some heavy issues—issues that meant she had to change the way she did business. Like me (three days earlier), she was in a quandary, confused about business and life in general. I told her about my intuitive coach's technique of holding a thought so I wouldn't create more negative energy around it. She knew I had a lot of things going on in every area of my life, but asked, "Could you hold the vision that this (situation) is going to work out to my benefit?" (We got more specific than this so that the Universe was clear on her intention.) Just hours later, the situation was resolved to her satisfaction. Is this magic? There may be a little divine pushing but one of the keys to this process is understanding what your vision is so that the reality can manifest.

An inner circle couple were really down because finances were tight for them, but they had plenty of energy to send positive thoughts about the sale of our house. They had no emotional attachment to our house selling, but had complete love for us and held the vision that my family and I were happy in all ways. So then I asked them, "What is it that you want?" My female inner circle friend said, "More money... security" (she was staying home with the babies, and was full of gratitude for this situation). My male inner circle friend (also her husband) chimed in, "Yeah, but not at the expense of me not liking what I do!" So I retorted (at the risk of giving advice when it wasn't asked for), "You've jumped around from job-to-job for a number of years and obviously aren't happy so what would make you happy and still allow you to pay the bills to your satisfaction?" After some discussions, they told me about a distributorship possibility where he would be his own boss and she could help build the business as well (over time). Both agreed that it was time to get specific on their vision for his (and eventually her) future career so we put some meat on the bones. "You will have the distributorship that will supply 'x' product within thirty days." I told them, "Let it go and I will hold the positive energy around it while you move forward on the logistics to make it happen. We will talk about this next month and you will be shaking your head at how easy it was to follow your dream." In this particular situation, within thirty days the product wasn't needed as they found that this wasn't the right opportunity for them.

What's interesting about this process is when you ask someone to pray, hold a vision, think happy thoughts about a challenging situation that they are not emotionally attached to, it can work (wording is important, so make sure your request or vision is clear). Those holding your positive vision(s) have no negative residue attached to your issue(s) and can truly send positive energy to the Universe. Prayer groups (in the mainstream) and Reiki remote healing (in the New Age spiritual circle) are great examples of this. Try this easy one-on-one way to decrease daily issues.

Cutting the Fat, Sharing the Load and Making Quality of Life Decisions

"Care and diligence bring luck."
—*Thomas Fuller, M.D., "Gnomologia" (1732)*

WHEN I HAD MY FIRST child, it broke my heart to go back to a corporate setting. I liked my work, I just hated to be away from my baby for such extended amounts of time. Plus my job required not only out of town trips, but travel out of the country. The first day I came to work, I closed my office door and wept. I called my husband and told him that I couldn't stand the pain. I was in such anguish that my body hurt. For forty weeks I carried her, and for six short weeks I nursed, lived and breathed her. Getting through the first couple of days, I dropped into an associate's office (not quite so perky) and an old school salesman was there and said, "Well, it's back to the real world." I rebutted, "The real world is at home!" I stayed home a little longer with my number two baby and nursed him a bit longer, but it was back to the office within eight weeks and my son spent his days with his older sister at a babysitter's. I consoled myself by saying that, at least, sister and brother were together. I was able to get some flexible scheduling, but when it came down to it, less time meant (perceived) less corporate commitment and being taken less seriously.

My last corporate job, I tried one more time to arrange a home/career balance and create a work-at-home arrangement two or three days a week. I had all the necessary office equipment so all they had to do was say yes. Dragging their feet, I finally forced an answer from my manager. He admitted that he backed another woman and allowed her to work at home and she ended up quitting anyway. Of course, now in his mind all women were "quitters." But this corporation lost out. I was a great employee with good ideas and was growing their businesses. Many don't see the benefit (nor do they believe it's possible) of people following their hearts as well as paying their bills. Many believe that you have to give up to gain. So I started my own company and arranged my schedule so that I could be with my family all the time. But I wasn't making the big bucks anymore and my husband was carrying the full (money) load for the first time in our relationship. We cut a lot of fat so that I could stay home and build a small business that would, eventually, provide a modest paycheck. The biggest reason for the change was to better our quality of life. It isn't always perfect but it works for our family.

As a business owner, I have merged efforts with a number of artists/ designers that are as interested in increasing the quality of their lives as they make a paycheck. Quality of life, of course, is about balancing body, mind and spirit. When I'm asked, "How do you do it?!" (raising a family, writing, running an international business, etc.), the answer is simple: I love what I do in all areas of my life! My life arrangement is a gift! But I don't do it alone, and I do it one day at a time. I have a great life partner, my older children help out and my youngest is a joy to take breaks with throughout the day. It continues to remind me of the "real (loving) world."

My husband and I have a great arrangement. The last two companies he has been employed by allowed him to have a home office. His company keeps overhead down and he's at home (when he's not traveling for work). Our youngest has even been able to toddle between our offices during the day to play. When her brother and sister get off the school bus, her arms fly up in the air to be picked up by her older siblings and off they go into rooms she's not allowed in during the business day.

When customers call, many are tickled when they hear my little one babbling in the background. Many know her by name. But it can be difficult to balance.

I notice that men (like my husband) who take their responsibility seriously as active, participating parents don't get the credit that they deserve from the masses. There is a real chauvinist approach to many children's books. Just pull a dozen off the shelf and see how much credit mom gets for raising the children in contrast to dad. Mom is cooking in the kitchen. Mom is cleaning. Mom is going to the grocery store and on and on.

My husband does the grocery shopping (mostly because I overspend when I do it), cooks, cleans (the rule in our house is one cooks and the other cleans) and we share laundry duty. He was at the grocery store doing his weekly shopping and a woman asked him if he did this often. He replied, "Every week." She came back with, "But you don't put the groceries away, right? He said, "Yes I do." She said, amazed and envious, "Do you have a brother?" I believe that one of the reasons why men don't share as many domestic responsibilities is (some, not all) women don't let go of doing the grocery shopping or putting away the groceries or separating the laundry or cooking the meals. When they don't critique the execution, and release their needs for perfection, it becomes someone else's responsibility in the household. There's an exception to every idea, but give it a try. (Women), try letting go of a domestic responsibility. It may not be done exactly to your standards and gentle coaching may be required for a time but everyone can be replaced, even you!

A friend was complaining that her husband never helped her clean the house. I had the same issue, was critiquing my husband's work, and actually going behind him to redo it. I did the same thing with my older kids, once I passed some cleaning responsibilities onto them. Talk about counterproductive and frustrating for both the cleaner and the critic. So, to accomplish what I set out to do and spread the wealth of domestic chores, I let it go. I let them do their jobs and if it wasn't perfect (in my eyes), I let it be. If it was really bad, I'd make some suggestions but have them make the improvements.

How can you increase your quality of life by sharing responsibilities? What do you need to let go of in order to achieve this?

Spiritual

"...Spirit is an invisible force made visible in all life."

—Maya Angelou, "In the Spirit,"
"Wouldn't Take Nothing for my Journey Now" (1993)

When People You Care about Don't Approve of Your Path

"Don't expect to be acknowledged for what you are; much less for what you would be; since no one can well measure a great man but upon the bier (a stand for a coffin)."

—Walter Savage Landor, "Lucullus and Caesar,
Imaginary Conversations" (1824-53)

WHEN I WORKED IN THE MAINSTREAM world of brand marketing I made a good living. My family and friends all "approved" and some even aspired to what I accomplished in the corporate world. But when I went into the body, mind, spirit industry it was a bit of an eyebrow raiser. I've taught a number of New Age spirituality

ideas and now even teach mainstream metaphysical (New Age spirituality) goal setting ideas of which I've now created a specific process. I've
promoted metaphysical (also known as New Age, conscious living, and
body, mind spirit) products and services worldwide and even published a
book or so. It didn't take long before it got back to me that a relative said,
"I can't believe she can make a living at selling that kind of stuff." Some
relatives poked fun at the ideas, products and (kooky) services and when
my first book came out, some feathers were ruffled within the conservative family block.

Following a path of a Catholic, being (mainstream) Jewish, or Lutheran
is much easier for people to accept because there are special books that
these folks follow. Even if people don't understand the details of your path,
the label creates some comfort. However, say that you're on a spiritual
path that doesn't have a finite name and you are forever a student. We are
supposed to have something to point to for the answers. "God" forbid
that we trust ourselves to do the right thing and consider our personal
word as gospel.

I read a death story from a gentleman with cancer. All signs of death
physically had set in but the hospital agreed (due to his belief system
regarding his physical body after his spirit had vacated) to allow his
physical shell to lie undisturbed for several hours. Mainstream medically
impossible, he came back to life after more than an hour, his brain and
body functioning to full capacity and his cancer gone. He had much to
share about his "death" experience but one piece struck me with an "ah
ha!" When he saw his higher self, he was one of many other higher selves
equaling one great big higher self. The higher consciousness is all of us
put together. We've heard the "we are all one," "we are a piece of God,"
"we are God," statements but this visual just made absolute sense. I'm not
here to convince you of an idea of what God or the Universe is, but if we

imagine that we are all a part of each other, how would we handle things differently?

It was only a couple weeks into summer equinox and I was making sales calls. I got on the phone with a store-owner who said, "I just love your products and can't wait to order them but I am relocating soon and need to make some heavy decisions to move forward..." Feeling empathetic and connected with her issue I responded, "This is the time to do it. You've spent time in the spring planting the new idea seeds and may have been in a bit of a state of confusion but now the earth energy is high and it will help push you along your way to execute your vision." The surprised store-owner said, "Where did that come from?" I replied, "Not sure." She went on to say, "I really needed to get this message from someone outside of my inner circle to confirm that I was moving in the right direction. I have to leave some people and things behind... So many people count on me... I'm worried that I'm not moving in the right direction..." I told her, "It's difficult to jump out of the day to day and be the visionary, but it's time to do this and by fall equinox you will be excited with the results." We ended the conversation with a "bless you" and a "talk to you soon." This person heard information that made sense to her. She trusted that she received the information in a way that could help her move forward which meant leaving people and things behind that no longer served her purpose. We weren't quoting any document, simply following a thought pattern of what felt like "oneness."

So how can we nurture our spirits, follow our dreams, climb every mountain, treat our inner voice with respect and use it as true guidance, and still deal with those we care about who are incapable or unwilling to understand any particular path?

First ask yourself, why do you find yourself caring about what this (previously) important person thinks about your direction? If you still feel the urge to expose yourself to this person or group, start taking physical notes on interactions where you feel supported and one with this energy and those where you don't feel supported and separate. This may take some time so be patient and truly understand what type of nurturing and deflating energy you experience in his/her/their presence. Be very specific because if you have an interest in being one with this energy, you will eventually share this information with the person or people as they may not be aware of your challenges in their presence. If they are aware and aren't interested in truly nourishing your spirit, again, why is this person or people in your life? Feed your soul. Encourage the health that being "one" brings.

Demonstrating Your Truth

> "God offers to every mind its choice between truth and repose."
> —Emerson, "Intellect, Essays: First Series" (1841)

MY CHILDREN WERE twelve, ten and two years old at the time and I thought it would be a good idea to expose my comfortably middle-class children to those needing a helping hand. Our first consistent commitment as a family entailed delivering meals to those unable to get out of their homes or prepare balanced meals for themselves on a regular basis.

Part of the training process required that I ride on someone's route for the day to understand the process. My trainers were a very nice, retired couple. The Sunday of my training, the husband came to pick up all the meals and paperwork and I got into his car to pick up his wife at church as she was teaching Sunday school. She got into the car, complaining about the preschool craft that she put together as she spent half of her previous week special ordering the supplies, buying baby food then emptying and cleaning the jars, and buying distilled water for this "easy" craft. She then went on to tell me stories over the past ten years of her deliveries, the homes, the people, who she was fond of, etc. Her husband was a master driver, getting us from house to house at, what seemed to be, lightening speed. Within an hour, it seemed like we were old friends. But then the penny dropped, "So Michelle, what else do you do with your time?"

Having no intention of sharing my spiritual beliefs, I had to decide within seconds, how much I was going to tell this retired couple, fresh off Sunday church (one was raised in the Bible belt of Tennessee). "Well," I responded, "I own an international wholesale gift company that distributes art products and I'm also an author." The same question was asked by her husband on the way to pick her up from church but he didn't feel the need to probe any further when I quickly transitioned him into talking more about his past career. But no such luck as she continued, "Really, what kinds of art do you sell and books do you write?" Well, the title of my second book is safer than my first so I mentioned *"Soul"utions* because the word "metaphysical" isn't in it. I then went onto talk about the art and jewelry (which was pretty safe). But, my new Sunday school friend probed further, "What's the name of your first book?" I had to respond, *Adventures of a Mainstream Metaphysical Mom.* A quick glance and statement from my (possibly) former friend said, "Metaphysical would definitely get my attention." Grinning I said, "It's not about being a witch or worshipping evil but about being okay with diversity and that all ideas basically lead to (or should lead to) the same path of tolerance, love and flexibility so we can live together in peace.... 'Metaphysical' is meant to get attention." The very quiet husband (who was a former owner of a business that was now run by his son, revealed to me before picking up his wife at church, and believer in incenting sales people with commissions and not base salaries) chimed in, "You gotta have a hook to get their attention. Sales appeal!"

The wife—more interested—added, "You know I have such a hard time teaching concepts from the Bible. I keep telling the children, these are just stories to teach you lessons that you can sort out when you are adults." She went on to tell me about a book she was reading about multi-cultural relationships as well and our two-hour training session came to an end. We embraced and said our good-byes.

I am continually exposed to the idea that people truly are capable of being open when they don't feel threatened or attacked. And when you do hold to your values, many people respond by finding a common ground. It doesn't mean that you have to agree, it just means that you are demonstrating mutual respect. When are you most likely to compromise your values or be fearful of living them at that moment? Is it in a particular group setting or with certain individuals? How can you gently demonstrate your values without the observer feeling threatened or attacked to live your truth?

The Lessons of Being Wrong and the Right in Wrong Doing

"Every mistake has a halfway moment, a split second when it can be recalled and perhaps remedied."
                    —*Pearl S. Buck, "What America Means to Me" (1943)*

I WAS FEELING VERY TASK-ORIENTED. It was the week before school. My oldest was in her first year of middle school. My youngest (one-and-a-half-year-old) was into everything within a blink of an eye, was hungry for information, struggling to communicate without words and just needed a lot of attention. My middle child, in the staging area for puberty, was still in elementary school (the only familiar ground for me at this point).

School supplies were purchased while the two older children were visiting their grandparents but my husband insisted that they choose their 3 ring binders. Not being able to scratch this task off my list was really irritating, but his position was the kids' binders are who they are for the entire school year. How could I even consider stealing their identities? Fighting my task-oriented need, I agreed to allow the kids to shop for their identity building binders for the school year once they got home.

When the kids returned there was absolute chaos. There was a ton of laundry to do, paperwork had to be filled out for school, checks had to be written for fees, and school clothes had to be purchased. Then we had to nail down new school processes like where and what time they had to catch their buses (now different times and places for two children). Blah. Blah. Blah. And an even bigger issue was developing, how am I going to keep an extremely active toddler busy while I manage my home business?

But back to the identity building school supplies, my husband said, "I'll take the kids to get their binders." I gave him strict instructions on what inch binders, zipper or non-zipper, etc. He came home with the wrong binder for one of the kids and that was all it took. I flew off the handle. My middle child began to get teary eyed because he figured it was his fault. My husband took the binder out of my sight so I wouldn't continue to rant and rave. My oldest was safe because she knew what she needed. And I had officially taken all my frustrations out on this $12 zipper binder and everyone that was connected with it!

Trying to get past my irrational behavior, the kids and my husband got on their bicycles and said, "Come on mommy, let's go for a ride (it will do you good)." Unable to come down from my flight of fury and unsure why I went into this rage to begin with, I couldn't allow myself to go at first. It was time to punish myself. I didn't deserve a family like this. I'm a complete maniac. What's wrong with me???

I finally got on my bike and rode with my family. They safely teased me a little but from a quick getaway distance in the event that I didn't take it too well. We talked. We played at a park. My husband rode next to me on the way home and said, "I'm doing the best that I can to help. I'll take the binder back." I swallowed my pride and finally blurted out my true concerns, "I just don't know how I'm going to take care of all of this. I'm stretched. And what's worse is I don't know how I'm going to take care of an energetic toddler and a home business (that I own and operate) and I just added nearly a dozen new sales representatives. I did this because I want to be home with the kids. I don't want to put our baby in daycare. What can I do?"

After more discussions, we realized that we had a friend who mentioned she wouldn't mind making a few dollars a week working from home. She had an infant and a toddler a few months older than our youngest and she had a holistic background (in addition to having a nursing degree). My husband happened to have his cell phone on him and said, "I know you can't wait. Call her right now (from the park where our kids were playing)." I did and she agreed to three days a week playtime for three hours in the morning. I could have lunch with my toddler then put her down for a nap in her own bed in the afternoon. By 3:00 P.M., my middle schooler would be home. And by 4:00 P.M., my elementary schooler would get off the bus. And a weight lifted from my shoulders.

It was lesson time for the children. I went onto tell my two older children that what they had to learn from this mental breakdown was to try not to do it. "Don't be like me and if you do I don't want to hear 'It's my mother's fault that I'm like this' excuse. I was wrong. I am feeling inadequate. I am feeling overwhelmed and concerned that I can't give each of you the attention that you need but we talked it through and have resolved a big piece of the problem."

It's tough to admit that you're wrong. It's even scarier for me to know that I'm going to see my children handle situations in the same way. Being a parent, you're looked to for answers. The vision I'm holding when I give the "Mommy is wrong" lesson is my lack of grace becomes my children's "I'll never do that when I grow up" position. I'm just going to have to swallow my pride as a spiritual being knowing that the answers might have to come from me being wrong and/or looking foolish so that others can learn how not to handle things in the future.

How can you be okay with the idea that you are, at times, supposed to be wrong in order for others to learn? A friend of mine told me that she has always said that she is just one big experiment. I can see her point.

Affirmations Working For and Against You

"A (wo)man's worth is no greater than the worth of his (her) ambitions."
—*Marcus Aurelius, "Meditations"*

MY HUSBAND, WORKING IN the computer world, came home after being out of town for a couple of days for work. Tired and a bit discouraged he said, "Well I got what I asked for. I affirmed to the Universe that my goal was to make sure that certain software processes ran through the client's system effectively. However, I didn't affirm that the output would be correct for the client (only that our software would run)." Back to the old affirmation drawing board!

Affirmation communication is a way to clearly state your intentions to the Universe. It's tough enough to do this on your own, but to have someone else affirm your goal that wasn't truly clear on what would fully be to your benefit could spell disaster.

Many of our neighbors boasted about the city councilmen living in our neighborhood and adjacent subdivision that gave us "voices" in our local government. Unfortunately, I, and many others, had some issues that were important to address (from our perspectives) and those government voices were on the other side of the issue. During a public meeting one of the council members said, "I understand the issues because I live in the same area...." But rather than allow him to misinterpret or misstate his understanding I spouted, "... you really don't understand the issues from my perspective..." It wasn't a very popular thing to say but his position incorrectly assessed the situation from many others' point of view. That affirmation, if allowed to manifest as truth, would have created a completely opposite result.

Do you have people in your life that finish your sentences for you or commonly say, "I know how you feel..." and go onto switch the subject and talk about "more important" issues (because your thoughts, obviously, aren't that significant or appropriate)? Maybe you have someone telling you that the way you express yourself isn't effective and he/she will speak on your behalf to shed a better light on your thoughts. When you allow this to continue, it creates energy that doesn't nurture or honor your thoughts and goals. It doesn't allow you to create an effective affirmation, specific to your needs.

In corporate America, I put my foot in my mouth many times. There were times when the way I handled a situation was irreversible. While my thought on the word "reverse" is a contradiction in terms because all things happen as they should, some lessons are harder to swallow than others. I worked for one brand marketing company that was extremely political (not so unusual) and from the day I walked into the door I was a fish out of water. Very few marketing folks liked my manager and were constantly discrediting what he did. He spent a lot of time "protecting" me from the corporate wolves (or so he affirmed). In order to get anything done,

I had to work around being protected and quickly gained the reputation for completing projects (which wasn't always the smartest political move). However, my manager was moved to another department and I was quickly reporting to the wolves who didn't like or respect anything my former manager did. I was one of his bad decisions so I was in big trouble.

It was a real struggle for me. On one hand, I wanted to be my own person. Speak freely. Make decisions. On the other hand, I was in an environment that fed on mistakes. In fact, a field sales manager told me that he felt really bad for me because all of my enthusiasm and creativity "would surely be snuffed out soon." Between people wanting me to make mistakes and notes being closely taken when I did make them, in the end, their affirmation of who I was became their "truth." I was mentally beaten in this company and left in less than two years.

There are risks to speaking for yourself and accomplishing your goals. Would you rather live by doing or coasting? Depending on your stage of life and employment situation, sometimes coasting is necessary but be careful to manage how the energy can spread to everything else you do.

Wanted: Soul Happiness, Faith, and a Bucket of Golf Balls...

"Man needs, for his happiness, not only the enjoyment of this or that, but hope and enterprise and change."

—*Bertrand Russell, "Philosophy and Politics, Unpopular Essays" (1950)*

I'VE ASKED MYSELF MANY times being full-time in the body, mind, spirit world (business, personal and pleasure), can you have clarity, live intuitively and be in the mainstream working world? I found it difficult getting caught up in others' competitiveness, filters, projections, judgments, insecurities, poorly designed floor plan layouts, sick buildings and the list goes on. For most of my mainstream corporate life, many of these issues were unconscious so I expressed my soul deprivation by getting sick (colds, coughs, stomach virus, pink eye…) or moody and "formal" (bitchy). I no longer have use for these tools and am rarely sick since I started my own business in 1997.

While it would have been easier and much less complicated to simply stay home with my children, volunteer at school and do mom networking, I decided to spend a bunch of my (and my husband's) money, and donate thousands of free hours to build an international body, mind, spirit focused company! Here was the Universe's job offer, "You have huge potential! Here's our proposal: work constantly to build this business and fork out thousands of dollars. In return you will have awesome life lessons and experience insurmountable expansion!" Next stop, additional partnerships!

My company partnered with artists, designers, authors, and speakers. While I knew (through past forecasting and business building experience) how long it would take to build my business and make it profitable (per artist, designer, author, etc. …) and this information was shared with those who joined my company, it was not always fast enough. Many thought they would be overnight successes. Others looked for a steady paycheck within six months to a year of entering the market (which I still consider "over night"). So a lot of people had come and gone, but those who truly held the vision of becoming an internationally accomplished artist, designer, author, etc., succeeded by continuously creating and living simply (or within their relative means).

I have had my days of uncertainty. I've managed to keep my head above water when orders were scarce and debt continued to mount, and I have observed others doing the same. For instance, there was a professional in the body, mind, spirit world who was quite accomplished in his craft but got angry at the world for wanting his work but not ordering enough to keep his financial situation stable. His (let's call him Sam) doubts translated to drastically changing his physical look, dropping his craft and he re-entered the mainstream job market to better his financial standing. He wasn't getting any younger, didn't have any kind of nest egg for retirement, and his debt had been out of control for decades, so it made mainstream sense.

Jumping back into this world, he was immediately exposed to gossip with the intention of damaging others' reputations, rumors, angry customers, angry suppliers and an angry employer when sales numbers weren't met. Then there was the, all too familiar, vibration of competitiveness and constant need for more that lingered in the background. Working long hours, it was difficult to focus inwardly and there was no longer space for an alter in his new uptown loft that formerly contained sacred stones and symbols. There was no longer "buy-in" on divine connections, prayer, meditations and ceremonies to better his financial or other life situations. "Soul"utions were on hold.

My children's great great uncle would send little messages to us (usually during the holidays) and one hung on our refrigerator for a long time. It said, "Believe in something." At this point in time, Sam lost faith and drastically changed his ideas on how he could truly achieve happiness. With this came additional ramifications: he was no longer having accurate visions. The work that he did chisel out time to do was no longer ethereal so he wasn't sure how they would sell in the body, mind, spirit industry and wasn't sure he even cared.

Was this because he was hanging out in the mainstream working world or because he was just simply unhappy with the way his life had been going for a very long time? Throughout his life, numerous family, marriage and professional relationships had gone bad. His unstable financial status started very early in life and he was in so much debt that he couldn't remember a time that he didn't have it hanging over his head!

A year after he went mainstream, he received a major promotion. Following this announcement, the owner of the business said, "You know you didn't have to make such radical changes in your physical appearance to succeed in this job." Sure, financially he was experiencing some success but his creative and spiritual expressions were in extreme imbalance.

Ethereal work was now impossible for him to produce, but Sam felt that he was as spiritual as ever. He was now enjoying golf regularly, was taking lessons to improve his game and had forgotten how competitive he could be. But there were additional subtle signs of imbalance as he regularly commented on how good he was feeling in general, when, in fact, he was getting sick regularly.

I've been there and constant cash flow is fun! My idea is not that corporate America crushes your spirit but that many can perceive it as a non-spiritual experience and "act" as such.

When in a mainstream work situation, how can you use "soul"utions to create a productive, yet serene environment? Have you ever felt like you need to do something extremely different to fit into a situation? What worked when you did this? What didn't work when you did this?

Challenging your "Emotional Intelligence" with the Seagull Strategy: An individual who flies in, makes a lot of noise, craps on everything, and then leaves

"A moment's insight is sometimes worth a life's experience."
—*Oliver Wendall Holmes, "Iris, Her Book,*
The Professor at the Breakfast Table" (1860)

IN THE EARLY 1990's a number of studies and books came out about "EQ" or Emotional Intelligence Quotient and how important it is for one to understand his/her own emotions and the emotions of others to act appropriately based on that understanding. This requires an empathetic, intuitive and, what some would call "feminine" approach to giving and receiving verbal and non-verbal communication.

To exercise and trust my EQ, I spread my wings in areas I was in charge of and had a sense of safety in. When it came to family matters, if something needed to be taken out of my child's reach, things were too quiet, or things were too noisy and a feeling of disaster was in the air, I acted on the premonition. Once confident I moved into other areas, like driving... should I zig or zag, what was that guy in front of me going to do...? As I continued to confirm my emotions or feelings as truth, I worked my way into more mainstream areas, the toughest one being business where "analysis paralysis" was a common dysfunction. Of course, numbers are important, but we can also make numbers look any way we want them to. Additional complications in business environments could include anger, fear, judgment, jealousy, frustration, and/or impatience that create a lack of clarity.

There are always going to be people that believe they know best or, at least, better than you day-to-day. It's like the negative traits of the seagull, those who fly in, make a lot of noise, crap on everything, and then leave. These people can bring out the worst in most everyone. And if you can't rise above this negativity quickly enough you become weak and defensive. These situations can even result in trying to cover up mistake(s) so that the seagull personality doesn't have concrete proof that he/she was right. This can ultimately result in a loss of integrity on your part. These people survive in environments where they rarely have to face their demons or failures. Failure, in this type of personality's world, is not about learning, it's about finding ways to point the finger in the opposite direction.

I work best with those who have failed and own it, as well as succeeded and share the credit when credit is due. It takes experience to make mistakes and if you aren't making mistakes you are simply standing still. Those are the rules for honest to goodness progress. Those with the seagull strategy can ask you to do some silly things. Then they accuse you of silly things once they've dug themselves into a hole. And watch out as they begin to fly away and blame others for their poor performance.

I was seagulled one day and after receiving the harsh "feedback" I thought, "Wasn't I supposed to see something like this coming? I thought my intuitive skills were sharper than that? What do I continue to do wrong?" I couldn't help but physically weep (in private) because I respected this person's abilities so I was careful to communicate that I, simply, was unable to handle the tough evaluation of my performance and straight-forward suggestions that followed for improvement. The seagull style also accelerated into accusations of not being true to my word, and all these assumptions were being made about my character as a result of one incident (without any recall of the history of past successes). My question became very direct, "Is this the end of our relationship?" The answer from the seagull was, "That wasn't my intent." So I licked my (hurt feelings) wounds and requested a more gentle approach in the future. Seagull approaches usually don't (fully) develop if EQ is being used as a tool by those exchanging thoughts, because empathy and respect as opposed to patronizing and criticizing are the primary patterns.

The seagulls can get you down but if you have the EQ to know that even the most irritating situations are life lessons to expand your consciousness, you are above the situation soaring like an eagle. On the flip side, ask yourself, when am I the seagull? Even if you only think seagull thoughts, consider it a seagull act because your mind closes, you become judgmental and negative. Relive how the person felt when you didn't have empathy so that you don't repeat this pattern.

Changing Lives through Observation and Listening

"When the oak tree is felled, the whole forest echoes with it; but a hundred acorns are planted silently by some unnoticed breeze."
—*Thomas Carlyle, "On History" (1830)*

I RECEIVED A CALL FROM a gentleman asking to book one of our partners and he opened with, "You don't know me but another retailer referred me to you... my store name is..." When anyone calls my company, I immediately begin searching for the company name in my database because, more than half the time, we know about them (they've contacted us before, we contacted them, they emailed us for some reason...). But this person's name and store sounded particularly familiar so I tapped away on my keyboard and, sure enough, he and the store showed up in another state and I asked, "Is this Rick from Mississippi" (bogus name and place to protect the not too innocent)? He, taken back, said, "Yes, it is but I'm no longer from that area. How did you know?" Responding with a bit of satisfaction I said, "I remember meeting you at a trade show. You ordered product, we shipped it but your wife returned it stating that you were in jail and you bought product that was not working for her store... I'm sorry, I'm not trying to get personal and I certainly felt like I was getting too much information from your wife at that time and this was several years ago..." He quickly responded, "Well, this is the fourth store I opened and I took a two-year hiatus and went on a vision quest and have done a lot of healing. Prior to this I also was co-owner of another store in Michigan called 'Elements.'" Another light bulb turned on and I quickly tapped in the name of that store to find that this was one of the few stores that ordered product from our company and never paid us for the goods. The store owner would never return our phone calls and when we did get someone on the phone we were told that she had been stolen from and was having a difficult time getting her financial affairs in order. Maybe I should have just politely taken his address and ended the conversation, but I couldn't help myself when I said, "Elements is one of the few stores that we did business with that never paid for the shipped product nor did she return it." Psychically feeling like he was squirming in his seat he went onto tell me that when he was married to her as well... "She wasn't spiritually going in the same direction as I... She was never a good business woman... I took the money... She kept the shop..." Torturing him enough and knowing that doing business with this gentleman was not a good idea, I updated his address in my files and felt like I should share this story because the plot thickens.

A couple of weeks later, I was following up on one of our company bookings and, somehow, we got into a conversation about "Rick." It turns out that he was undercutting other body, mind, and spirit stores in the area. He knowingly scheduled major events directly before established events in the area in an attempt to overtake the market. And he was married yet a third time (at least in my database)! Regardless of the accuracy of all the "he said, she said," it was more than interesting to observe this person's path from a safe distance. It almost felt like I had a taste of being on the other side watching a movie and guessing the plot.

The divine humor and drama that accompanies business is endless. The store that Rick was involved with in Mississippi has gone down in the history of our company as the strangest reason we accepted a return. The store in Michigan was one of the few stores that never paid for goods shipped (and it was only $75). Why did the Universe connect us? I didn't know this guy from Adam and yet I had the past ten years of his life documented in my head and database. It was like a "This is Your Life" segment titled "You can run but you can't hide." It really wasn't up to me to interpret, nor to judge. However, I wasn't all that eager to send him a catalog on our products and services. Even though there are two sides to every story, it was definitely time to acknowledge that this person has a pattern (or is exposed to a pattern) that was not conducive to doing good business.

I was chatting with an independent contractor that I'd worked with for a number of years. I asked her how her husband was doing. He was a member of The Union, his job had been threatened for some time and they were experiencing many ups and downs. Just by chance, I said, "You probably don't know about the manager of XYZ company…" And she quickly jumped in and said, "Oh, sure I do, he really offended one of my husband's co-workers." I said, "Really, did he tell you why?" She gave a general explanation on how my manager friend didn't support The Union… and I said, "Let me clarify the situation as I believe I heard it. My manager friend was leaving the building for an appointment and two Union men stopped by unannounced saying that he should not advertise with certain local media because they don't support The Union. My manager friend can be a bit direct and said, 'I support the freedom to make a choice…' And the two Union members basically said they would tell everyone his position (of not supporting the Union) and that he 'better watch his step.'" I went on to say that, "I wasn't there, but my manager friend called me on the same day a bit shaken by the confrontation." I can tell you that I did get a few of my facts crossed because I wasn't there and my independent contractor probably got only part of the story as well, so adding some caution to the communication process, who would have thought that I would be so tightly knit into a circle of people and events that I had little to do with?

We truly don't "get away" with things that have negative impact. It may not be returned in the same form (like someone getting direct revenge). It doesn't mean that you're going to be punished by "the devil." But it seems like our souls bookmark energy exchanges and they reopen chapters at the appropriate times. The same holds true for positive exchanges, you experience rewards in many forms. Can you think of instances where you've participated in, received and/or observed events and days, months, or even years later it has additional impact? How can you positively observe, listen, participate, and expand in the full synchronicity experience?

Increasing Your Quality Time... No more passing the buck!

*"We do not live an equal life, but one of contrasts and patchwork; now
a little joy, then a sorrow, now a sin, then a generous or brave action."*
—Emerson, "Journals" (1845)

IT WAS MY FIRST "Forgive, Remember, Move On (Let Go)" semi-
nar right before spring equinox. I overheard a woman talking to her
friend in the bathroom who said, "I'm either going to the 'letting go' or
'feng shui' workshop." I was freshening up and couldn't find a brush and
commented, "One of these days I'll remember to bring my brush..." and
she offered, "Use mine." Doing what I insist my children never do, I ran
her brush through my hair and said, "I'm the one teaching the 'letting go'
class" and she responded, "I wasn't going to go because of the numerology information. I feel like people don't empower themselves when they
use tools like these. They blame their astrology sign or their numbers for
their issues..." Only having about five minutes to gather my thoughts and
materials for my talk, I told her that we would spend about ten minutes
on numerology and the rest would be on the subject of letting go. Then
I hurried off to my assigned room.

In order to forgive, remember and move on, you have to have an idea
of what to let go of. To conjure up the emotion (which would include
anger) and pinpoint the issues, on this particular day, I asked people to
assume that they were responsible for everything that has happened or
will happen in their lives. Ironically, my hairbrush acquaintance raised
her hand and said, "Excuse me. You mean to tell me that if a three-year-
old child is abused that it is all her fault?" While I was about to explain

that, "It's all your fault" was about finding the anger trigger points so that we could zero in on "letting go" areas and take us to the other side of empowerment, my mouth opened and the word, "Yes" plopped out. I went onto say that this was how we were going to work toward letting go in this workshop and I'd understand if she needed to leave (again, wondering if those words had actually come out of my mouth). This same woman had just given me a short lecture in the bathroom on how people don't take responsibility for their lives, but obviously wasn't ready or willing to go to the next level of taking complete responsibility for her own, if just for a moment, to try and understand what is in her way of spiritual progress. She left the room and I regained my footing by asking if anyone else felt the need to leave to do it now so that we could get on with the class. I didn't realize just how lucky the rest of the class was until later.

Another author, speaker, friend happened to see me chatting with my hairbrush friend outside of the restroom. Following the event, I told her about the discussion and abrupt departure during my workshop. She responded, "I know who you're talking about. That same person was in my workshop and took a chunk of time being argumentative and holding up my class as well…"

Providing me a little relief from the day's drama of actually suggesting that someone leave my lecture, we drove home that night and stopped for dinner. My youngest daughter (not even two years old at the time) had outpatient surgery scheduled in the next few days and I was explaining how unhappy I was that she had to experience this at such a young age. There was a black mole on her knee since birth and the doctors recommended that we have it removed (medical precaution). Hesitating to say the "C" word, our waitress overheard our conversation and said, "I have cancer! I had cervical cancer, weighed seventy-three pounds, actually died on the table but I was revived." Dumbfounded as we listened, she went onto say,

"I have three children... now have a tumor in my intestine and have to do more therapy to get rid of it. I know what to expect and I know I'm going to get through it." I asked how much time she would be taking off work and she said, "I'll have to work while getting my treatments." When she left the table we both just sat there, intuitively suspecting that she wasn't going to make it through, and breaking out of the silence my friend said, "You know, I really don't understand why things happen like that. Can it really be our choice to suffer so intensely?... My (current) teacher said it isn't our choice..." One of my class attendees that same day asked me, "A friend told me that it will take seven lifetimes before you can get rid of a particular karma, what do you think about that?" My response, "As a higher source (a parent) to your daughter, would you make her relive a problem for a set number of lifetimes? What is the right number? If you embrace a Universe of free will, how could there be a finite number attached to working out issues?"

But who really knows?

We take steps constantly to enhance or destroy our lives. When we don't exercise, or we smoke, or we eat unhealthy food, is this someone else's will? We live in a world of "who to blame" and we become victims! We have people who are overweight trying to sue fast food restaurants because they can't control their eating patterns. And taking the victim pattern to another level, people are suing tobacco companies, and the government is taxing cigarettes then using the sin tax money to balance their budgets! What's wrong with this dysfunctional circle? Many refuse to take responsibility for what they are doing to themselves or others. So why not, just for a minute, pretend like everything that's going on in your life is a result of your choices so that you can pull your life together?

Upon leaving the restaurant, we settled up the bill and I said, "Don't worry about leaving a tip." She looked down and said, "Why did you do that?" looking down at the twenty dollar tip on the table (for a twenty dollar meal). I responded, "Why do you think?"

While there are many who see that their lives are crap because of someone or something else, lots of people have suffered through life experiences knowing that they will evolve stronger. Do we consciously look forward to suffering? Do we really think the harder the lesson the better? Do our physical bodies look forward to pain? Do we want to see our loved ones in pain? Only if you're a threat to yourself and those around you!

I continue to hold a vision of gentle lessons everyday. However, there are incidents that make us wiser through experience instead of hearsay. Think back to when you were a parent or being parented. I can't remember how many times I told my oldest daughter as a baby, "HOT, NO NO!" and pointed to the top of our stove. But until she experienced the burn and had a mark on the palm of her hand that looked like the grid of the top of our stove, she didn't totally get it. Did it please me when my daughter experienced the terrible burning pain? No, I could even feel her pain! Did she become wiser? If she didn't she would be in for a world more of pain.

What destructive patterns have been difficult for you to break? How many times did you have to experience a pattern that was destructive before you broke it? How did you break the pattern? What has been your observation with others alleviating destructive patterns? How loudly does the Universe or your Source have to shout before you get the message (this would mean a friend pointing something out, your doctor or lawyer, messages on the radio or television, your dreams...)? Increase your quality time in this lifetime by breaking destructive patterns and taking full responsibility for your life and getting it sooner than later and/or more gently than harder.

Social Outcast or Independent Thinker?

"Better starve free than be a fat slave."
—Æsop, *"The Dog and the Wolf" Fables (6th C. B.C.?)*

As I've gotten farther down the road of independent thinking, published my first book to encourage diverse thinking, expanded my body, mind, spirit company, I still have to continue to remind myself of the physical aspects of living in a mainstream community where healing work generally means being a doctor, nurse, or medically measurable assistance of some sort. I accept modern medical advice, but alternative approaches are also a part of the equation in my household.

We happen to have a large population of doctors, nurses, and other medical professionals in our neighborhood and one of my intuitive partners came to visit and said, "You know Michelle, people in this neighborhood are going to think you're really odd and generally won't accept what you do for a living." While I shrugged it off as part of life (i.e., people will judge others), there were times when I felt that spiritual common ground would be a nice thing to experience every now and then.

A friend called me one night and kidded with me saying, "So and so stopped by this afternoon to give me an invitation to her home products party next week, did you get yours?" I responded with relief, "No." I could tell that my friend was a bit taken back by the fact that she had gotten an invitation and I hadn't and transitioned nicely into, "It said to bring a friend. You wanna be mine?" My long "no" included how "the winter cycle has been very good for me and my creative juices were really flowing (which meant that I didn't feel quite as social) and I was writing a lot of material for my workshops, and my next book, plus I was reading a couple of books but thanks." After I hung up the phone I thought about how my kids go through these struggles of being invited or not invited to functions and what a "hurt fest" that can be. And, just for a second, I wasn't sure if I wanted to be invited so I could turn it down. But it is something that you have to expect as an independent thinker.

As an independent thinker, do you become a social outcast? Are you destined to simply be alone? I'm reminded of what independence means to me when my toddler came into my office and grabbed my hand to pull me away from my desk. I felt the warmth of her lovely little hand, dependent yet independent, leading me to the treat drawer. En route, I realized how the simplest interaction from my inner circle became my strength and continuously fed me with the confidence to be my own person. I surround myself with people who enjoy me and/or love me for who I am.

What is frightening about being an independent thinker? List those who would enjoy your company just because it's your company. List those you are exposed to regularly (and must come into regular contact with) that don't appreciate your independent nature. List three reasons why your independence is more important than this/these persons'/peoples' approval(s). Remind yourself of why you love your independent self.

One Independent Thinker's Terrific Day

"Happiness depends on ourselves."
                              —*Aristotle, "Nicomachean Ethics"(4th C. B.C.)*

So how does one independent thinker and potential social outcast have a great day? It was "Good Friday." To the Christian community this is a sacred day marking the day that Jesus began the rebirthing process, and we were having a Spring Egg Hunt on this day. It's been a tradition for us since our children were very small. We have friends from many religious practices, so we ask everyone to check their belief systems at the door and enjoy the rebirthing of spring together.

It was a glorious day. It was not too hot and not too cold. There was plenty of cloud covering so that the eggs containing chocolate wouldn't melt. I slept in a bit, had a little breakfast and went to my scheduled reflexology appointment. This massage therapist was very good as she not only massaged my feet, but put warm towels behind my head and kept one foot toasty with warm towels as she worked out the kinks of my opposite foot.

Floating on air on my way out, I wished I could walk on my hands so as not to spoil my foot pampering. In complete quiet in my vehicle, I drove home in a very relaxed state. When I got home, I had a light lunch and went outside and hid plastic eggs filled with candy. We had nearly 450 eggs to share with our friends and neighbors and no possible way to really hide the eggs so I decided to just toss them all over the yard. My husband got a little tricky but gave up after only a couple dozen eggs and our front and back yard had colored specks everywhere you looked. My rationale, better they find them now so we don't find them while doing yard work.

Nearly thirty children showed up for the hunt. While it took three of us about a half-hour to disburse the eggs in our yard, it took less than ten minutes for them all to be found. Kids were opening eggs, trading candy, drinking juice and parents were yacking and sneaking a couple of their favorite sweets.

Within an hour, all our guests were gone and we had an easy clean-up. The baby went down for a nap within the hour and I had some free time and decided to do a little shopping by myself. On the way home, I stopped by to say "hi" to a friend. I made it home in time to pick up the family so we could go out to dinner together. The kids were well-behaved, the baby was entertaining us and herself enough for us to have a nice meal. We took a family walk after dinner. Still early, I had some time to go out shopping again (to qualify this, I don't like to shop but today was different) so I called a girlfriend on a whim and said, "I'm going to the bargain clothes store." She said, "Is that an invitation?" I said, "Yep." And off I went to rescue my friend who had been stuck in the house with her toddler and infant all day. She ran out of her house with a smile and we were off.

I didn't try anything on. My girlfriend was planning on losing some weight and was going to reward herself with new clothes once she did this. So she was grabbing things, telling me how cute this and that would look on me and what looked like my size. Never, ever do I do this but, we narrowed it down to about a few blouses and we agreed that I could try them on at home and return them if they didn't work out—we were being bold on this night.

Not ready to go home, we decided to get a really fatty dessert and hot cocoa. Between the eating, drinking and continuous talking, I'm not sure we were actually breathing.

By 10:30 P.M., we decided to go home. The baby was in bed by the time I got home, the older kids were watching a movie and I was completely happy. I played with my family, my kids shared their spring ritual with other kids in the neighborhood (and it only took one painless hour), and I got to play with some of my inner circle friends.

When reflecting on this day, I was amazed by the perfect balance from my perspective. I wasn't looking at it through anyone else's eyes but my own. I was completely in the moment of quality interaction without concern for judgment.

Ask yourself, "What kind of perfect day can I put together for myself?" What's stopping me from doing this regularly? How often is regularly?

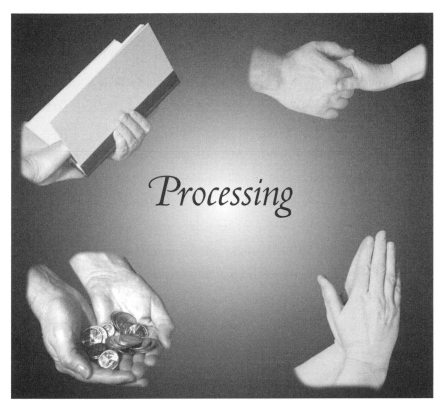

"Many of the insights of the saint stem from his experience as a sinner."
—*Eric Hoffer, "The Passionate State of Mind" (1954)*

Introducing Soul Nourishment

"The soul is the voice of the body's interests."
—*George Santayana, "The Life of Reason:*
Reason In Art" (1905-06)

I WAS TEACHING A CLASS FOR A MAINSTREAM organization combining feng shui and mind, body, spirit goal setting techniques. The objective was to set goals and enhance their lives by reflecting their goals within their environment. We had a small class and I had some new material and was in for a great teaching and learning ride. Trying not to be too invasive, following a goal setting exercise, I asked for top-line goals from each attendee. Touched by all the students' stories, I had to hold back the tears when I found out that one (soft spoken but extremely committed to spiritual healing and changing her life) had a chronic condition that zapped all of her energy for days at a time. She only found out the name for her thirty-year condition six years prior to attending this class. Coming to our class was a major feat for her as she rarely left her home. Highly educated, she got her bachelors, masters, Ph.D., got married, gave birth, held down a high caliber job for many years, all the while assuming that she had some mental issues or chemical imbalances that just made her different from everyone else. She asked herself "Why am I so depressed? Why don't I have any energy? Why do I lack enthusiasm?" Yet her numerology (an analysis included in this class) indicated that she was a natural conversationalist that could reach her life potential by matching her natural ability to both express herself and to listen, with her ability to be creative. It also indicated that her creativity in self-expression was very high (writing, painting, sculpting, music and/or writing).

When I met her, she was very unhappy. She left an area (to relocate for her husband's company) with many friends and a home she loved to find no friends, and a house she hated (interior issues as well as exterior). She felt isolated especially when her health issues would arise and lived on property that encouraged privacy versus social interaction.

Another student had gone through a two-year transition to end a romantic relationship and was set on breaking her old patterns with dead-end life partnerships that didn't allow her to express herself as the individual that she held the vision of being. Plus, she wanted to follow her heart and pay her bills creating a home business!

After hearing these stories, I had a mild twinge of not being good enough to coach these women down their paths. I did a quick prayer to ask the Universe for the strength to mediate them through the process of setting goals and making changes in their environments that would make their lives flow more effortlessly. While these women were different ages, backgrounds, and had very different social preferences, they had strong links in overall vision. They were looking for answers to change their lives and upgrade it. They shared uncertainty and fear of possibly not being able to achieve happiness that they'd observed outside of their inner circles. And to make changes, they all had to embrace their personal power to nourish their spirits. Working with these women and many others, I've found a way to identify patterns and areas in lives that create discontent. This process has been successful for many people and brought their lives into balance which, in turn, creates happy, exciting, beautiful lives.

To quickly summarize two of the mentioned students: Our lonely, unhappy, sickly student now has small get-togethers that include creating greeting cards and other items to clear clutter in her craft area while enjoying coffee and good chocolates. She has developed a small women's group and conserves her energy so that she has more good days than bad. The other ended her dead-end relationship and has a very successful home business with several people now working for her.

There are no hard and fast rules for success. We are all individuals, but what if we could access some tools to point us in a direction of happiness and soul fulfillment? We've been given a number of questions to ponder throughout this book. Let's talk about some processes that can tie it all together.

Being Your Personal Visionary

"Our plans miscarry because they have no aim. When a (wo)man does not know what harbor (s)he is making for, no wind is the right wind."

— *Seneca (4 B.C.-A.D. 65)*

L IFE USUALLY ISN'T ABOUT just one area of life that's a bit messy. Our lives aren't that linear. Soul nourishment ultimately requires a process to push you in the optimal direction, I call this "soul mapping." Many times one issue materializes and then it inevitably bleeds over into other areas of life. It can be intimidating and feel nearly impossible to accomplish balance, so let's reprogram that thinking and talk about the:

TOP 10 TIPS TO BEING AN EFFECTIVE SOUL MAPPER:

1. Go with the flow once you know what body of water you should be drifting in.

In the New Age industry, "go with the flow" is a term that we throw around frequently and it serves us as long as we get around the river bend with as few bumps, bruises and mouthfuls of water as possible. When I go on vacations, I make sure basic needs are met: a clean, safe place to stay; convenient places to purchase food; activities for the kids, etc. (social/intellectual/spiritual). Then I go with the flow.

When running a business, basic expenses must be met, profit goals are targeted, debt must be managed effectively (finance). Essentials have to be met before going with the flow and flow it will.

2. Write it and it will come… Record your goals by area of life on paper to gain clarity.

There are simply too many things to remember in a given hour, day, week, month, year. How can you possibly remember it all? In addition, how can you keep the information straight, concise and clear? You can't unless you take the time to write it, review it, edit it and commit some keywords to memory to stay focused. Let's not make the excuses that "Spirit, God, the Angels or the Universe will provide." Definitely keep the faith, but exercise your right to "free will" as well.

3. Share your goal(s) with those close to you to help you stay on course.

Elect a personal coach(es) to remind you of your goals. For so many years, I ran my business and my life rarely asking for help. I decided to ask my business-savvy husband to look over my next 3-year business plan, current business action plan, as well as my soul mapping plan, and asked him if they felt realistic. He gave me feedback, I made changes and now I frequently ask him for advice and how he sees them connecting to my soul map plan.

4. It is written, but nothing is in stone. If you have new information, change your path.

This may feel a bit contradictory, but we do the best we can with the information that we have at the time. From a process standpoint, your top line document (depending on your stage of life) may stay the same, but how you get there can change drastically. Allowing changes and new opinions, promotes growth.

5. Know the difference between a long-term vision and short-term tasks.

If written with soul, your long-term vision will change very little but how to achieve goals will change because your life shifts as you age, as life partners change... financially, intellectually, physically, socially, and spiritually.

A technicality but very important distinction: your long-term vision is your umbrella statement per area of life that you will generally live by. Everything else you write is how you get there and the tasks.

6. Reward yourself for progress as much as humanly possible.

We spend so much time beating ourselves up for our weight, a financial blunder, messing up a relationship, not exercising the way we should… we forget that for every negative there is a positive. Celebrate the baby steps. My children have a chart on the wall to measure how tall they are. One of my children was having issues with body type. I kept telling her that she was in her puppy stage and certain things are going to be out of proportion for a while then "poof!" she's going to go through a growth spurt. Thank goodness she did! Otherwise there would be heck to pay for the rest of this lifetime: "You said I would grow! It's all your fault!" She still remembers the seasons, the years, how many inches she grew in a matter of a few months as well as how much she weighed.

7. Evaluate your strengths and weaknesses in relation to a goal(s) regularly (especially when in frustration mode) knowing that all things happen for a reason.

Evaluate weaknesses, ultimately turning them into strengths.

8. Do not evaluate your accomplishments by comparing yourself to others.

You will never be happy if your vision is to emulate someone else's life. Certainly, we learn by experiencing and our experiences revolve around other people many times, but do things because it serves you. If you're just trying to keep up with the Jones's you'll be "trying" this entire lifetime.

9. Focus on your vision. This is not your significant other, co-workers' or children's plan. It is about you (they can be included if it's beneficial to you).

Be selfish! This is your plan to be happy.

10. Do not spend time creating your plan then put it in a drawer.

If you don't see the value in using this as a tool then stop now. If you do, once you create your short and/or long-term plans, shrink it down to a size to carry in your wallet, calendar, planner, put it on your refrigerator or frame it and put it by your desk to serve as a constant reminder of your goals.

Reprogramming Your Reality... Soul mapping and balancing

"The absurd man is he who never changes."
—*Auguste Barthelemy, "Ma Justification" (1830-31)*

IMAGINE YOU ARE IN your car and are waiting for the traffic signal to say "go." The person behind you isn't paying attention and bumps you from behind, right at the very moment you were taking a drink of soda pop. The soda pop spills all over you. Visualize reacting negatively—the yelling, the anger and the response of the person that hit you. Now visualize playing back that moment in time and visualize changing the story in ways that serve you more effectively—you acknowledge and handle the problem as an accident and not as "on purpose" and the response of the person that hit you.

Imagine how positively reprogramming situations impact your life in the moment and in the future. If it's more physically finite (you've lost a loved one, you've been physically incapacitated, you've lost your job, etc.), allow yourself to imagine the positive impact, opportunities and growth you and others experience over time (but first allowing yourself time to work through the grieving, anger, and processing). For instance, maybe you had a terrible physical ordeal, were hospitalized and suffered to great lengths. But, in your suffering, you were able to learn many new things, meet new people, decide on a more fulfilling life path, impact others' lives positively, became spiritually advanced in the face of physical trauma, and/or appreciated the gift of physical life. The objective is to reprogram your negative reality into one that progresses you forward in the future. Thinking from a negative or positive perspective makes it so.

Let's break this down into smaller parts to get a handle on how we can look at this in every area of our lives: Financial, Intellectual, Physical, Social and Spiritual. Let's identify where life is in and out of balance and focus on how your overall life nurtures your spirit. Let's look at ideas to help us connect to this concept of balance by:

- Keeping It Soul Simple (KISS);
- Creating action steps for more challenging goals (Techniquest);
- Understanding the "Personal P's" for more challenging goals (Personal Product, Positioning, Pricing and Promotion);
- Evaluating personal progress;
- Integrating these personal processes into your life (like a good diet and regular exercise) to manifest your ultimate reality.

In *Adventures of a Mainstream Metaphysical Mom*, you were introduced to the concept of writing an Areas of Life Mission Statement with top-line ideas on how this might clarify your life direction. The following pages will take you into more details on how to do this and additional processes connected to your everyday tasks and overall development.

All of the above-mentioned concepts fall under the umbrella of "soul mapping." FIPSS processing is one of the core organizational ideas to gaining insight. This is an acronym for Financial, Intellectual, Physical,

Social and Spiritual development. Depending on your personality type and preferences, you can walk away with a one-page statement that could be interpreted as your personal 10 to 15-year philosophy depending on what life stage you're in, or a simple action plan that focuses on tasks for the moment to get life on track.

For instance, by your mid-twenties to early-thirties, if you have children, your world would revolve around one life style. You adjust to becoming an empty-nester maybe in your fifties and then are entrenched in retirement and grandparenting duties from there. Your soul map would be very different for each stage of life financially, intellectually, physically, socially and spiritually. While this concept is best executed when not under the gun, the reality is people wait until things go bad before they pursue clarity. Each area of life is categorized as follows:

FINANCIAL: Career, Business, Wealth, Savings, Budget, Retirement

INTELLECTUAL: Gaining Knowledge, Life Direction, Spiritual Education, Training, Travel

PHYSICAL: Exercise, Eating Habits, Health

SOCIAL: Reputation, Fame, Inner & Outer Circle Events, Volunteer and Non-profit work, Physical relationships

SPIRITUAL: Relationships (primarily non-physical), Family, Self, Inner Child, Creativity

If you want to move some of the categories around a bit that's fine. Just be clear on how and why you defined it differently. Now let's look at some situations and personality types as examples in this process.

"IN A RUT"

Cindy owned a business that paid her bills but it was the same old thing and lacked excitement (Financial and Intellectual). While she had been dating someone exclusively for nearly three years, it didn't look like he was ready to make the ultimate commitment of marriage anytime soon (Social). She seemed to catch viruses on a regular basis and one infection had gotten so bad that she was bedridden for nearly two weeks (Physical and Spiritual). She had employees but when the last one left, she didn't recruit any new talent to save a few dollars (Financial). On her free time, she simply floated around in her apartment pool and connected with a friend or two but was really only waiting for her significant other to show up (Social). While her intention had been to exercise a few days a week, she was just plain tired (Physical) and many commented on how sickly skinny she looked (Physical).

"Burnt Out"

Brenda, the dynamic volunteer, had been chairing major (non-profit and social) events for a number of years (Social). Although she'd made some great money for non-profit organizations, made sure her children were participating in sports and other activities and had many acquaintances, she was burning the candle at both ends and she had no time for herself (Spiritual). While she made time to go to the gym and watched what she ate, she wasn't sleeping enough (Physical and Spiritual). She couldn't remember the last time she and her family sat down to a meal together and never knew when her husband would be in town (Social). She never felt like she could relax, let her hair down and have a little fun (Spiritual). Reading? What is that (Intellectual)?

"Burnt at the Stake"

Reba, the relocated, moved from an area she really loved to a quaint town because of a job opportunity for her husband. She had visions of community support, neighborly greetings as she walked through her subdivision, little coffees with like-minded, and intellectually stimulating friends (Social/Intellectual). She had less traditional life ideas, however. She felt her neighbors would not appreciate her "outside the box" thinking and would result in her son not being invited over to play (Social), so she kept her ideas to herself. Her son was old enough to be in school and it was time for her to think about going back to work and doing something that was fulfilling (Spiritual/Financial) however money was not an issue. She found that she was regularly depressed (Spiritual) and held the vision that she could find outlets to make her happy (Spiritual). Her back was giving her problems and she found that she had days where she simply could not get out of bed (Physical).

As various people process, one of the frustration points may come up, "Who am I to think that I can truly manifest a reality that makes me happy... Putting soul visions to paper would simply prove that I am failing. I will never truly be happy."

Let's play a game and assume that we each have the inner knowing to manifest our life stories. No research required. To visualize or brainstorm our lives, first we must realize the 5 steps to our personal power:

1. **Intuition is truth.**

Remember that fear does not equal intuition. "Burnt at the Stake" made assumptions based on fear about what her neighbors would think of her and how they would treat her son. When she took a step back from the perception, she realized that she didn't have to wear her less traditional ideas on her shirt sleeve to acquaint herself with parents of similar aged children. She developed a small inner circle of friends and they would congregate/socialize and discuss freely and without judgment.

2. **Everything happens for a reason.**

All experiences lead to your "divine plan." The smallest lessons usually have the largest impact. "In a rut" continued to get sick because she needed to reflect on her relationships and business. As she continued to ignore that both needed major attention in order for her to move forward, she would catch still another virus.

3. Having gratitude manifests a constant flow of good things in your life.

Get the most out of tough lessons and answer "If I have to be unhappy for the moment, how can I be unhappy as gently as possible?" "What will being unhappy accomplish?" This certainly doesn't mean don't grieve, or get angry... but it does mean find the lesson or silver lining as much and as soon as possible to pull you out of the darkness. "Burnt Out" had to grieve the loss of time with her family, her husband and her self. It was natural to look back but she learned to have gratitude for the experiences and the awareness of what was truly important in her life.

4. You are empowered with choice to reach your destiny.

There are many roads that lead to the same divine plan (happy and unhappy). "Burnt out" was looking for enlightenment in non-profit organizations because she was temporarily unable to find it at home. However, when she cut down rushing by decreasing time commitments, combined physical exercising with self-awareness processing, she was sleeping more soundly and felt rested. She even attended a few seminars and started reading a couple of books to further her growth.

5. Do it now or Do it later

Breaking destructive patterns will set you free, save you time and increase your learning curve. "Burnt at the Stake" had to be completely honest with her self. While she was afraid to own thinking outside of the box, at this stage of her life, this pattern no longer served her. Now her dance card is full (fulfilling her personal need for more social interaction) and she has a small inner circle of friends that socialize regularly to safely discuss the "other" subjects. Interestingly enough this social/spiritual group keeps getting larger.

For the moment, let's own that we are the source of power that can manifest an extra-ordinary reality and move onto the next idea, "Keeping It Soul Simple."

KISS… Keeping It Soul Simple

"The ability to simplify means to eliminate the unnecessary so that the necessary may speak."

—*Hans Hofmann, "Search for the Real" (1967)*

SOME CAN SEE THE BIG PICTURE right away. Others see details and tasks much easier. One isn't better than the other, it just is. Sometimes it's easier to look at the tasks at hand to create daily simplicity so let's look at this idea. The goal here is to give your overall tasks meaning for the year. The format looks like this:

KISS LIST (KEEPING IT SOUL SIMPLE)
THIS YEAR'S MEANINGFUL TASKS-AT-A-GLANCE

Financial

Get paid $_____ per month by _____ .

Decrease debt to $_____ or less by _____ .

Company dollars gross $_____ by _____ .

Intellectual

Attend three formal training classes by _____ on how to fine-tune my intuitive capabilities.

Physical

Personal Trainer once a week. Walk, Yoga, ride bicycle, roller-blade or treadmill mix at least three times per week. Effective Immediately.

Spiritual

Meditation or connect to spirit through ready-tation three times per week for 15 minutes minimum per session. Effective Immediately.

Social

Have adult time (no children) once every three months with an inner circle friend or new acquaintance to expand my learning through personal contact.

Spend adult time one time per month with my life partner, focusing only on our relationship (outside of our home). Effective Immediately.

When I do individual sessions, I ask my clients, "What is good in each area of life and what needs improvement?" Seeing these two ideas on paper gives us a good idea of what areas of life are most out of balance, helps prioritize tasks, and creates additional action steps. Remember that we do the best we can with the information that we have at the time. As you write, know that this is a guideline to get you to the next level until more information is presented to you over time, so don't put it off. It's a big step to get rid of your meaningless tasks or personal clutter. This document will change regularly, but it promotes awareness of what your overall goals are for the year in each area of life.

In some cases, further processing would be helpful. To do this, you may want to consider an action step process or "Techniquest." Techniquest is defined as an empowerment technique to guide you through your ever-changing journey. Remember we've already established that you have all the information within you (five steps to personal power). To serve as an example, look at the before-mentioned "Spiritual" KISS task of "meditation or connect to spirit through ready-tation three times per week for 15 minutes minimum per session. Effective Immediately."

For some, the KISS list is as far as the analysis needs to go but if you remain at a standstill, break this down into even smaller attainable pieces. Getting quiet seemed pretty straightforward. Less than one-hour out of 168 for the week seemed more than attainable but most people can't sit quietly for one-minute without being intimidated with the process. You can write a simple task list to achieve the goal of "meditation or connect..." or add one more layer called the "Personal P's" to the "Techniquest" process.

The "Personal P's" literally translated are Personal Product, Position, Price and Promotion. What is the physical or final product? What position of power does that put you in? What is the price to pay to attain that product and position? Once achieved what level have you evolved to? These categories are very helpful when you get stuck because you're answering open-ended questions about the situation (almost like you're interviewing yourself). For additional clarification, here are some examples of Personal P's.

Personal Product — Ultimately the vision or final product you are manifesting. Your opportunity(ies).
— I am in the perfect job by (3 months, 6 months, 12 months...)
— I have a long-lasting, monogamous relationship by (3 months...)
— I am diverse and experience many countries, people and cultures by (3 months...)
— I am debt free by (3 months, 6 months, 12 months...)

Personal Positioning — Internalize your visions and they become you.
— I am the best person to do this job
— I am trusting and trustworthy in all my relationships

— I am expanding my awareness and learning about the world as I travel when and where I like to go

— I have a constant flow of money and am debt free

Personal Pricing — This is fear many times. Is there a price to pay emotionally or physically? Do you have equity in a position that you've taken? Let it go. This is the only way you can move forward.

— What if I can't do the job?

— I am not always honest and trusting so how can I be trustworthy?

— No-one else travels the world. I could use a new car instead so people can see my "success." I can't afford to travel!

— I am in debt and living beyond my means. No way am I debt free!

While there are compromises and give and take, turn these fears into positive manifestations by living them to the best of your ability.

— I am successful and am moving this/my business forward.

— I am a catch in my romantic relationship and trust that I receive the same respect as I give.

— I have a constant flow of money and am debt free allowing me to travel when and where I like.

Personal Promotion — Live your vision to raise body, mind and spirit to a higher level. Progress!

— I am experiencing success in business that nurtures my body, mind and spirit.

— I am experiencing a romantic relationship that nurtures my body, mind and spirit.

— I am experiencing my trip to Jamaica in June that nurtures my body, mind and spirit.

To get a bit more detailed, and make this more of a living example:

AREA OF LIFE (FIPSS)
Spiritual

ACTION

Meditation or connect to spirit through ready-tation three times per week for 15 minutes minimum per session.

ACTION PLAN (3 month, 6 month, 3 year+) utilizing 4 Personal P's

○ **Personal Product**

3 month… Everyday verbally say "My intuition is truth."

6 month… Meditate 15 minutes, three times per week and get to know and trust my guides and understand their processes.

12 month… Meditate 15 minutes, three times per week and ask my guides/angels/God to take me on journeys to open me to continuous Universal knowledge and growth.

○ **Personal Position**

Internalize my goal/vision, with patience knowing that I am a part of God and have access to Universal wisdom to live a full and happy life in the physical as well as spiritual in this lifetime.

○ **Personal Price**

3 month… Nothing

6 month… Fear that I will fail at accessing my guides and can't trust my intuition.

12 month… Take 100% responsibility with what happens in my physical life as a result of my intuitive choices (and every choice is an intuitive choice regardless of how "measurable").

○ **Personal Promotion...**

Live the vision that I trust my inner (intuitive) self without question. I have complete access to all Universal wisdom at the time that is right for me.

TIMING FOR HAPPINESS (Always have a deadline and take baby steps if need be)

In 3 months (by month/year) celebrate the ease of acknowledging my intuitive self

In 6 months (by month/year) celebrate my non-physical relationships and acknowledge them as my physical guides/ teachers as well.

In 12 months (by month/year) celebrate the empowerment of choice and the lessons.

Again, the "KISS list" may be as far as you need to go (or can tolerate). But I have noticed, when I feel like a part of my life is out of control and I write my ideas out in a bit more detail, I feel a weight lifted and sense of power.

Your Long-term Life Vision

"A rock pile ceases to be a rock pile the moment a single (wo)man contemplates it, bearing within (her)/him the image of a cathedral."
—*Saint-Exupery, "Flight of Arras" (1942)*

THIS IS THE MOST ADVANCED step in the soul mapping process because it takes long-term vision to create this one-page document. You would see this process as valuable if you have long-term concerns that require perseverance and have a habit of thinking farther out than one year or have an underlying philosophy or value system that you would like to continuously reinforce in this lifetime. You will not fail if you choose not to tackle this. It is simply another idea to create balance in a mainstream metaphysical conscious living life.

You'll notice that this process is less task-oriented and more "overall theme" like. Here is an example of a long-term soul map utilizing the FIPSS concept:

FINANCE: Celebrate success but be flexible to allow for family focus. Be creative, honest and profitable with a goal of making a gross income that supports a comfortable retirement and supports our children's development to adulthood. Keep things on a loving level.

INTELLECTUAL: Travel with and without children. Listen and learn. Pay attention to and completely trust my courageous, "fear-less" inner self. Live spiritually and provide the same opportunities for our kids. Speak gently and with love.

PHYSICAL: Exercise regularly on my own and with my family. Strike a realistic balance of good foods for me and my family.

SOCIAL: Initiate, with ease, gatherings of family and friends. Allow others to organize events as well and be active participants. Be active and reliable school and (local, national, international) community volunteer but still know when to say "no." Involve my family in volunteer work.

SPIRITUAL: Love, cherish, and be thankful for the moments. Listen, respect and appreciate family, friends, work partners and internal and external customers. Follow my heart and my fear-less intuition. Laugh at myself to bring the best out in me. Find goodness, unity, truth and beauty in all things. Slow down, be patient, pay attention. Keep things on a loving level.

I highly recommend that you work with the task-oriented process first to connect the FIPSS concept to your direct experiences. This will reveal to you whether a long-term approach would serve you as well. Once you do this (and only you can determine the appropriate timeframe), begin tackling your 10–15 year, or life-long soul map one area of life at a time. This could take days, weeks or months.

How do you get there? Light some candles. Turn on some soft music. Have plenty of fresh water (no food or beverages outside of water is suggested as it's distracting and can become mind altering). Find an alone space and do these three straightforward exercises:

1. Venting Exercise. Make a list of one to five bullet points of things that currently make you unhappy in each area of life. After each unhappy thought write "Date: "

2. Gratitude Exercise: Make a list of one to five bullet points of things that currently make you happy in each area of life.

3. Visualization Exercise: You're looking into a parallel world at yourself in the perfect life. Brainstorm through writing or audio recording what this reveals (ultimately getting to a written document). You're reprogramming negativity and, no matter how ridiculous, you are rewriting your reality. Sometimes the negative will come out so go ahead and process it, but turn it around to your benefit. You will then go back and highlight the pieces that could be edited into your long-term vision. Write with soul purpose!

4. Turning Task Into Visions: Take a look at your KISS list and Techniquest action steps processing. Can you find longer-term vision from the tasks? Compare the long-term vision example given with the KISS list, can you see how these relate?

Once you've completed these long-term soul mapping exercises, go through all written material and use a highlighter and mark all of the key words that reflect vision. Take a close look at your "unhappy" list, next to "Date: " put a finite month, year that you anticipate this negative manifestation can be turned around or alleviated from your life (this may or may not make your long-term list). Record deadlined goals on a separate piece of paper and consider adding this to your personal calendar. Use the "bigger picture" words to build your statements for each area of life. Post this, along with your KISS list, in a place where it is regularly viewed by you.

Metaphysical Quarters and Season Changes… A time to evaluate your life

"The changing year's successive plan / Proclaims mortality to man."
—*Horace, "Odes" (23 B.C.–15 B.C.)*

So now, in theory, you've written your major tasks for the year. There may be a few items in your KISS list that could use further processing to help you accomplish your goals and you've used the action step or "Techniquest" process and the Personal P's to clarify your steps to success, and you may even utilize the long-term vision process. Transitioning into every Equinox and Solstice, the energy naturally shifts, and as a result, you will intuitively be ready to make changes and analyze progress of achieving your extra-ordinary reality in December, March, June and September. Energy levels feel: contemplative and reflective for winter (approximately December through March); rejuvenating and fresh for spring (approximately March through June); high, upbeat and in total swing for summer (approximately June through September); harvest-like (of all preparation from December through September), chaotic and preparatory (in the sense of preparing for the winter), and finally festive (multiple holidays, harvesting crops of ideas) for fall (approximately September through December). More explanation about the cycles of the earth and how they influence your energy, moods, physical and spiritual life can be found in *Adventures of a Mainstream Metaphysical Mom,* but here is an analysis format to consider.

STRENGTHS/WEAKNESSES REVIEW
EQUINOX/SOLSTICE EXERCISE

Priorities for Month: _____ Year: _____

Spiritual

Projects/Actions:

Meditation or connection to spirit through ready-tation three times per week for 15 minutes minimum per session. Effective Immediately.

Strengths:

The ready-tation versus meditation process decreases the traditional pressures of meditation making it a realistic process to connect to spirit in a mainstream, mother, business-owner life when I don't put too much pressure on myself.

Weaknesses:

Sometimes, 15 minutes, three times per week seems unattainable. I take too much preparation with pillows, just the right place, monitoring external noises, etc... and it turns out to be an hour plus fifteen minutes and once I get there, I don't know what to do, how to communicate, who to speak to, and what the messages mean. Meditation doesn't seem like a realistic spiritual process in my life at times.

Once you've taken a closer look at your strengths and weaknesses you can adjust your ever-changing action plan to overcome your weaknesses.

There are many other energy influences to consider when going through this type of personal processing. What personal year you're in, your destiny number, your astrology influences, your birth order, and all the everyday mainstream muck can be factors. To integrate these personal processes into your life (like a good diet and regular exercise) and manifest your ultimate reality:

1. **Follow The 5 Steps To Realizing Your Power**

Intuition, Synchronicity, Gratitude, Choice, Now or Later (see page 195).

2. **Prioritize To Optimize**

Decide what are your number 1, 2, 3 priorities then take them one step at a time.

3. **Write It And It Will Come**

Once it's in writing it begins to manifest so be careful what you ask for (you're sending the message to your subconscious and the Universe)!

4. **Reward Progress**

5. **Evaluate To Improve Today & Plan For Tomorrow**

No one is going to be happier for you than you. Have gratitude for your progress and evaluate your lessons to make improvements in the future (in prayer, meditation, formal writing exercise, etc.)

Add this all up and what do you get? You experience:

• where your life is in and out of balance (FIPSS);

• simplification by "Keeping It Soul Simple;"

• pro-active life patterns by creating action steps for more challenging goals;

• healing and personal problem solving skills by evaluating personal progress and revising patterns to manifest success.

What's Your Short-term Number?

"What is the life of man! Is it not to shift from side to side?—from sorrow to sorrow?—to button up one cause of vexation!—and un-button another!

—Laurence Sterne, "Tristram Shandy" (1759-67)

THERE ARE MANY ENERGY influences to consider when setting goals. I have found numerology useful in determining what type of energy is surrounding me as a result of my birth date, birth name or current name. I use this, not as something that rules my life, but as something that may give me more insight into my current and future situations. When I work with clients and conduct workshops, I have been known to look at numerology as a type of spring board. In the soul mapping process, as we visit "goods" and "bads" in each area of life, if there are certain life challenges, many times, we will find specifics in your chart. For instance, an "8" personal year attracts a constant flow of money. One of the life challenges connected with this number is money seems to flow out as quickly as it flows in. So creating action steps to catch some of that money before it flies out of an "8" year would be beneficial.

It's helpful to know what kind of energy surrounds you as a result of the year you are in. Your personal year number gives an indication of the trends and circumstances you may experience during a particular year (the short-term by my definition). Your personal year cycles are based on the Universal year cycles and therefore usually run concurrent with the calendar year but may intensify around your actual day of birth.

There are nine personal year numbers, which makes up a complete Epicycle. Each Epicycle reveals the progression of your growth. The "1"

Personal Year indicates your first steps in a new direction. The years that follow indicate your progress along this path, concluding with your "9" Personal Year, which completes the cycle and then you start all over again.

Here's how to calculate your personal year utilizing your birth date. The objective is to get the number down to between 1 and 9, for example:

2003 (is the current year you are calculating)

+ 5 (August 15TH is your birth date = 8+15 = 23 ‡ 2+3 = 5)

= 2008 (intermediate sum)

2 + 0 + 0 + 8 = 10 ‡ 1 + 0 = 1 (calculate down to single digit)

Personal Year = 1

PERSONAL YEAR 1— New Beginnings & Opportunities (Spring/ Summer Vibration):

A year of creation, in year one, you are setting the tone for the next nine-year cycle of your life. Not to scare you too much but everything you do now will affect your future (no pressure). Don't hold back. Take charge of your life. This is the year of major changes so be decisive. Start new projects. It's prime time for new goals and birthing of new life ideas: a new way of eating, a regular exercise program that you can stick to for a lifetime, new learning/studying/reading, and new relationships. Post these goals where you will see them everyday (words, pictures, symbols) to help manifest your new reality.

There may be some emotional adjustment for the first two or three months but your body, mind and spirit are simply adjusting to the energy that comes with many of the upcoming changes and work to be done. So be open-minded, organized, and focused. The time is now to set the tone for the next major cycle of your life. Have courage and keep a clear head to make the best decisions.

PERSONAL YEAR 2 – Patience & Tact (Winter/Early Spring Vibration):

A low tempo year, this is the time to be a bit more cautious, contemplative and nurture your plans, ideas, and/or projects. Situations that develop this year will, likely, put you on the defense whether it is a real threat or simply imagined. This is a good year to lay low and associate, for the most part, with your inner circle, soul mate(s)/group (particularly when discussing plans). This may disorient you, at first, as you will be unusually sensitive and vulnerable and your drive and momentum will be much different from last year.

Be patient and use your listening ears especially when frustrated or depressed. With confrontations on the rise, subtle but delicately direct prodding, tact and cooperation will keep you moving forward. Don't let this disrupt your focus but, remember, being forceful is not your best approach this year. Post the words (or symbols) "compromise," "win:win," and "cooperation" on a board where you will see it everyday.

It may feel like you are constantly struggling, but there are many opportunities to advance your plans, however it will be slow going. Take this "inner time" to read, research and quietly create.

PERSONAL YEAR 3 – Social & Light Hearted (Summer Vibration):

This is a high-energy year, time to expand and have fun! This is an upbeat time of personal expression, creativity, and artistic talent. You are lighthearted, dynamic and charismatic and drawn to social events (including possibly increased travel). This is a great year to entertain and be entertained. You may meet new and exciting people, but be careful not to create a year of chaos that totally obliterates your discipline and focus. Symbols, at eye level, that may help you positively reinforce this year could be creative artwork, pictures of true friends and fun travel.

It is easy to be optimistic, enthusiastic and have gratitude this year.

Friendships are strong. Exciting people are more likely to materialize. Finances are solid. This energy can speed up projects as long as your enthusiasm is based on real world manifestations but requires solid direction and concentration.

Enjoy, celebrate but balance with focus.

PERSONAL YEAR 4 — Building Blocks & Accomplishments (Fall Vibration):

A time to reap the harvest after planting (year one), nurturing (year two), and growing (year three) over the past three years, this is the time to be organized, practical, detailed, and realistic. Coming off a high-energy year, your concentration and ability to focus will be much improved. You may receive recognition and support from your inner circle as a result, but more importantly, you will have a feeling of great accomplishment (a return for all your focused work).

Remain flexible to take full advantage of the, sometimes surprise, opportunities that present themselves. Perseverance, focused work, foundation, and versatility are the words for the year (post building block symbols at eye level to remind you of the energy of the year).

It is a good year to build foundation: buy real estate; remodel your home; make sound investments as result of practical research; take care of postponed projects.

PERSONAL YEAR 5 – Constant Change (Late Spring/Early Summer Vibration):

Ready, Set, Change! Hold onto your hat because many surprises will come your way and it is a very lucky year. Be open and ready to embrace new opportunities. This is a year to take intuitively calculated risks (weighing facts with gut checks) and be quick of reflexes. It's a time to promote yourself, to travel and, possibly even, change residence to take full advantage of the upcoming opportunities. Symbols to consider (although you may not be sitting much this year) would be those of luck, adventure, and new ideas.

It's out with the old and in with the new and a great energy to experience following struggles last year. Some mistakes will be made but this is bound to happen when you can't apply old learning to new situations. Be careful to not overindulge in the physical (over eating, excessive drinking or drug experimentation, being promiscuous, or overspending).

PERSONAL YEAR 6 – Balancing Personal Growth & Relationships (Late Winter/Early Spring Vibration):

Although many opportunities are blossoming, the energy may feel contemplative as well, this year requires that you go within to optimize your personal growth as well as bearing the burden of others' issues. It's a time of progress, financial advancement, major career opportunities and new responsibilities coupled with inner work issues of domestic responsibility and attention needs of family (including your relationship with your significant other) and those in your inner and outer circles. It's time to think with your heart and make sacrifices, be a comforter and caregiver, find your place in the community and help others. It will take much discipline to create an atmosphere of harmony and balance in so many areas of life.

You have the empathy energy of year six to deal with all of these issues effectively. The symbols to apply to your daily life are those of love, flexibility and gradual growth and expansion (a flower in the process of opening, rain showers in spring to coax growth...). Ultimately, doing this type of soul work brings renewed relationships, often a birth in the family (where appropriate) and major birthing in other ways.

PERSONAL YEAR 7 – Solitude & Rest (Winter Vibration):

This year is about you and your inner growth. This is your time to be alone, go (from an etheric sense) inside and find answers to better understand yourself. The three "R" symbols applying to this year are Reading, Rest and Relaxation (deities, relaxing/low stress environments with warm/nurturing colors...). Others may see you as anti-social or disappearing off the face of the earth but if you don't acknowledge this energy, particularly with physical rest, your health could be at risk. This doesn't mean that you won't be able to address daily duties, regular exercise regiments and responsibilities, it simply means that you are in a "student state" with your course of study being inner-self.

There will be many synchronicity events inspiring you to take a closer look at life. An opportunity is there to experience the joy and beauty of life and is purely presented to you by the Universe/God/Spiritual Guides/ Angels/Buddha... for the growing awareness of self. The energy of this year brings many things to a standstill (allowing you to do your reflection work completely) and can be disconcerting. But too much concern for the material will turn this period of your life into a very bad experience and you may find yourself wondering what you did to deserve this if you fight it.

PERSONAL YEAR 8 – Material Rewards (Fall Vibration):

It's harvest year! The effort you put out in the past seven years will equal that in rewards. You are efficient and focused. Your power, mental creativity, vision and intuition are at a major high. After last year's long rest and reflection period and, possibly, doubts about the state of your business or career, you will find more empowerment energy. You see the light at the end of your financial tunnel. Checks are received. Promotions come through. Business deals close.

As long as you've had the opportunity for inner growth during the soul-searching of a seven-year, you will find yourself more clear and focused and able to pursue and reach your financial goals. Again, because rewards are directly proportionate to your efforts and motivations, this year could also end up in loss, bankruptcy and failure. This isn't an exam that you study for in one night. It's a process of life experiences that result in gain over time.

PERSONAL YEAR 9 — Out with the Old, In with the New (Spring Vibration):

It's out with the old to make room for the new. We're preparing for new plantings. Time for completion, bringing to a close all unfinished business. Clean house of problems, strained relationships, stressful situations at work, pay off old debts (material and karmic) and physically purge things that no longer serve your higher good but could be useful to others less fortunate. Your symbols for this year would reflect space, cleanliness, and freedom of all things keeping you from moving forward.

Clearing your body, mind and spirit clutter encourages complete freedom, social and accelerated creative energies but this requires that you face problems and overcome them. This will take courage and strength and is not going to be an easy year as you face the fear of letting go. However, once addressed, you will feel relieved and on the brink of a positive breakthrough by the end of this year. This is the end of a nine-year Epicycle. Enjoy the cleansing process and the weightlessness!

The Personal Year information is a combination of reference material from my personal studies and experiences as well as references from professional numerology reports licensed through Hans Decoz based on the work of Hans Decoz and Tom Monte that I utilize for individual sessions and workshops. On the internet, do a keyword search on "Decoz" for more information on his numerology work.

I went back over twenty years to track life landmarks with personal years and it was a very interesting exercise.

2003 – 1 Yr.—New Beginnings & Opportunities

- *Adventures of a Mainstream Metaphysical Mom* wins national award (now the neighbors are really talkin')
- Company turns a profit
- Committed to regional and national non-profit work

2002 – 9 Yr.—Out with the old, in with the new

- Moved to new home (first time built a home)
- Published *Adventures of a Mainstream Metaphysical Mom*

2001 – 8 Yr.—Material Rewards

- Started building new home

  (IRS windfall of money allowed us to pay cash down-payment)
- Birth of third child

2000 – 7 Yr.—Solitude & Rest

- Pregnant with third child

1999 – 6 Yr.—Balancing Personal Growth & Relationships

- Introduced my company nationally (birth at International New Age Trade Show)
- Re-aligned company objectives and partnerships
- Much formal training in New Age concepts (1998 & 1999)

1998 – 5 Yr.—Constant Change

- Quit mainstream job
- Committed full-time to building new company but did at home to be home with family (completely new learning and daily processes)
- Reading and practicing New Age concepts and ideas more closely

1997 – 4 Yr.—Building Blocks & Accomplishments

- Established/created new company

1996 – 3 Yr.—Social & Light Hearted

- Moved to new city (first move away from where raised as a child) for a new job opportunity and made many new friends/acquaintances

- Began exploring "New Age" spirituality

1995 – 2 Yr.—Patience & Tact

- New job opportunity closer to home (decreased daily and national travel)

1994 – 1 Yr.—New Beginnings & Opportunities

- Left long-standing job for new job opportunity (but not a good match—commute was two-hours per day, and increased travel)

1993 – 9 Yr.—Out with the old, in with the new

- Birth of second child
- Regular travel international and U.S. for work
- Baptized for the first time with my second born

1992 – 8 Yr.—Material Rewards

- Pregnant with second child
- Major expansion at existing job

1991 – 7 Yr.—Solitude & Rest

- Moved to "upgraded" home (for a really great price)

1990 – 6 Yr.—Balancing Personal Growth & Relationships

- Birth of first child

1989 – 5 Yr.—Constant Change

- Pregnant with first child

1988 – 4 Yr.—Building Blocks & Accomplishments

- Bought first home
- New job opportunity in Product Marketing

1987 – 3 Yr.—Social & Light Hearted

- Got married

1986 – 2 Yr.—Patience & Tact

- Graduated college
- New job opportunity in corporate Public Relations

- Got engaged (soul mate year!)

1985 – 1 Yr.—New Beginnings & Opportunities

- First paid internship with advertising agency (first "real job")
- Moved out of apartment with boyfriend (now my husband and life partner)
- Moved into an apartment with a few girls to experience college life from a different perspective

1984 – 9 Yr.—Out with the old, in with the new

- Changed college major (again)

1983 – 8 Yr.—Material Rewards

- Landed a better paying job to get through school and maintain transportation (my own car)
- Changed college major
- Moved in with my boyfriend (now my husband and life partner)

1982 – 7 Yr.—Solitude & Rest

- January 1982, first date with my now life partner and husband (met in French class)
- Recovering from financial hit of driving an uninsured car (life in a bit of a standstill or, at least, not very mobile)

1981 – 6 Yr.—Balancing Personal Growth & Relationships

- Graduated high school
- Started college
- Major car accident, nearly took my life (right before first quarter mid-terms)

This exercise may be helpful for you to familiarize yourself with the energy of each year (in theory, you'll experience each year about ten times in this lifetime).

What's Your Long-term Number?

"As wise women and men in every culture tell us: The art of life is not controlling what happens to us, but using what happens to us."
—*Gloria Steinem, "Revolution from Within" (1992)*

THE MOST IMPORTANT number in your numerology chart is based on the date of your birth, the date you entered your physical life. While you have your own unique character, there are certain energies that surround you that can influence the way you interact within this lifetime. Embracing the idea of a Universe of free will, you have ultimate freedom to do with your life as you like and the Life Path number gives a broad brush look at opportunities, challenges, and lessons you could encounter in this lifetime.

In the soul mapping process, as we visit "goods" and "bads" in each area of life, if there are certain life challenges, many times we will find specifics in your chart. For instance, an "8" life path may not like to be told what to do, at times. One of the life challenges that can be connected with this number is to learn to be part of a team, and understand that to listen and learn is also a part of leading. So the "8" could benefit from positive social interactions (depending on what else is contained in his/her chart).

Here's how to calculate your life path utilizing your birth date. The objective is to get the number down to between 1 and 9, 11 or 22. For example:

1963 (year of birth)
+ 5 (August 15th is your birth date = 8+15 = 23 ‡ 2+3 = 5)
=1968 (intermediate sum)
1 + 9 + 6 + 8 = 24 ‡ 2 + 4 = 6

Life Path = 6

The following information is a very short summary of each life path for general planning purposes. To really get into the nuts and bolts of your life path and a full interpretation, you would benefit most from obtaining a more detailed report.

LIFE PATH 1, THE LEADER

Rely on your inner strength and independence. This will allow you to become an effective leader and/or creator. This will result in your ability to satisfy your material needs and achieve a position of status that satisfies you.

Beware of the potential to be too self-absorbed. Others' opinions will be beneficial to your growth. Silence can be golden.

Your Path is the same as:

Martin Luther King

Emperor Napoleon

Peter Tchaikovsky

LIFE PATH 2, THE SILENT PARTNER/PEACEMAKER

Perfect your ability to quietly persuade as you are a peacemaker and diplomat. Your sensitivity to the feelings of others will be a great asset in many situations and you are often the power behind the throne. This allows your ideas to grow as a result of others' support and ownership. This will result in people seeking your advice behind-the-scenes, allowing you to develop and receive loving relationships.

Beware of the potential to be frustrated as others take credit for your ideas. Realize that this is a part of your learning as your ideas won't survive without the support of others with additonal influence. Your balance is to take an active role without being the leader and be willing to take a back seat without appearing apathetic or indifferent.

Your Path is the same as:

Bill Clinton	Wolfgang Mozart
Jacqueline Onassis	Ronald Reagan

LIFE PATH 3, THE CONVERSATIONALIST

Match your natural ability to both express yourself and to listen, with your ability to be creative. Your friendly, social side results in others feeling welcome and comfortable. This will result in people admiring you and seeking you out as an enjoyable companion. Your special talents can enable you to excel in areas of creative self-expression (writing, acting, painting, sculpting or music).

Beware of the potential to becoming too frivolous and possibly superficial. If you are unable to express yourself fully, you may withdraw, which will change your mood drastically. If others hurt you, your artistic way with words can cut like a knife.

Your Path is the same as:

Hillary Rodham Clinton	Jodie Foster (actress, director/producer)
Bobby Kennedy	Jonathon Winters (comedian)

LIFE PATH 4, LIVING IN HARMONY

Live in harmony with limitations (environment, body, opinions). With patience and hard work, you will bring order where it, possibly, did not exist before. You're honest, sincere, and responsible and have a strong opinion on what's right and wrong. This can result in a positive expression of great courage. The negative expression would be extreme stubbornness.

Beware of feeling frustrated by your limitations as you are making it more difficult on yourself. You can be bossy and dominant. If you create chaos for yourself, this is the total opposite to your path and will result in total discontentment.

Your Path is the same as:

Franklin Roosevelt Jr.   Babe Ruth

LIFE PATH 5, UNENDING TALENT

Learn how to handle freedom responsibly. Your quick wit, enthusiasm and eternal youth allow you to do many things well. Your challenge is to spend your time wisely. Moving from one place, person, job, and adventure to another will become less fulfilling over time. Patience and sticking to a task will allow you to experience the satisfaction of completion. Getting on track can take some time, but your growth will be phenomenal!

Beware of feeling overwhelmed by the many opportunities that present themselves. Because the excitement of something new keeps you going, you don't notice the frustration that others may have trying to keep up.

Your Path is the same as:

Helen Keller   Abraham Lincoln

Steven Spielberg   Mao Tse Tung

Vincent Van Gogh

LIFE PATH 6, THE RESPONSIBLE ONE

Accept the responsibility of serving family and friends. You are capable of balancing situations and are generous, sympathetic and kind. This will result in much friendship and love in return.

Be aware of the difference between helping and interfering, those who truly need care and those who lean on you. Once you have mastered this, you will have a clear sense of when to serve and when not to. Express your own individuality despite the responsibility you carry.

Your Path is the same as:

Rev. Jesse Jackson   John Lennon   Stevie Wonder

Pope Paul VI   Eleanor Roosevelt

LIFE PATH 7, WISDOM AND FAITH

Become aware of non-material forces—knowing yourself, understanding your intuitive side, finding faith, peace and the deeper meaning to life. This will help you to become easier to get to know. You'll be less reserved and more likely to trust and be trusted and be more adaptable.

Be aware of your struggle to let go of the material pleasures to follow your path. To conquer this will bring you into other pleasures of wisdom and faith. Only then will your life have true meaning for you.

Your Path is the same as:

Muhammed Ali   John F. Kennedy

John F. Kennedy Jr.   Bruce Lee

Marilyn Monroe   Sugar Ray Leonard

LIFE PATH 8, THE MATERIAL MASTER

See the benefits of the material world and the power that comes with mastering it. Your ambition, self confidence, energy, realism and good judge of character will position you for an executive role.

Be aware of the single-mindedness that comes with goal-oriented realities. You could misuse power and become intolerant with people resulting in resentment. If your material accomplishments do not result in personal happiness then your lesson has not been learned.

Your Path is the same as:

Bob Dole   Nancy Reagan

John D. Rockefeller Sr.   Elizabeth Taylor

LIFE PATH 9, THE HUMANITARIAN

Understand the deep satisfaction of giving without reward or return. Your ability to have compassion for the world, your broadmindedness, tolerance and passion, help you to become the selfless, non-materialistic person on this path.

Be aware of your potential difficulty believing that selflessness cannot be fulfilling. You will satisfy some of your materialistic needs, but will find little satisfaction. This can be a difficult lesson as it can seem less empowering to believe that when you give to others it all comes back. Rewards to those who can follow this path are endless.

Your Path is the same as:

Jimmy Carter   Mahatma Gandhi

Carl Jung   Norman Rockwell

LIFE PATH 11, THE INTUITIVE

Learn about the spiritual world and how it relates to the material world. This is a master number and means you have additional awareness, unique abilities and understanding. To reach your potential, you must learn to trust and develop your own intuition to tune into the beyond. You should involve yourself in psychic or occult studies.

Be aware that you are rare and can be difficult to deal with. You are so aware and sensitive that everyday life may bring many pressures that others never feel. You have huge potential, but may have difficulty turning it into something practical in the physical world. If you decide to back away from your gift(s), your energy will take on Life Path 2 traits.

LIFE PATH 22, MASTERING MONEY & HUMANITY

Learn to combine financial mastery and work for the benefit of mankind. Practical and charismatic, you are on a unique wavelength. You're capable of rising to the top of your profession.

Beware of feeling overwhelmed by your power or giving into your selfish desires. You may accomplish some goals, but not receive the lesson. Try to harness your nervous tension. If you decide to back away from your gift(s), your energy will take on Life Path 4 traits.

Your Path is the same as:

Woody Allen   Bill Gates

Elton John   Mark Twain

Oprah Winfrey

The life path information is a combination of reference material from my personal studies and experiences as well as professional numerology reports, licensed through Hans Decoz, based on the work of Hans Decoz and Tom Monte. I utilize this for individual sessions and workshops. On the internet, do a keyword search on "Decoz" for more information on his numerology work.

Reaching Your Goals with the Five Senses

"The secret to success is constancy to purpose."
—*Benjamin Disraeli, "Speech" (June 24, 1870)*

THE SIMPLEST THINGS YOU SEE, feel, touch, smell and hear influence you and those around you in very big ways. Here are some top-line suggestions of how to reach your goals utilizing your five physical senses. Depending on your life experiences, personality, profession, education, social, and spiritual goals, these may be mixed and matched and are only a few ideas that might reinforce your focus.

Symbols, Key Words, Affirmations and Color to reinforce your goals

	SYMBOLS	KEY WORDS/AFFIRMATIONS	COLOR BALANCING
Financial	• Money, Gold, Silver, Royal colors • Successful Friends/Relatives • Jade and other plants that have quality jewel names • Fine Jewelry • Quality clothes • Quality surroundings	• I have a constant flow of money • I am financially secure • My money grows every day • Money is always there	• Blues to relax and expand (the deeper the color the more relaxing) • Greens for financial and material success • Black for power and career • Neutrals show understanding
Intellectual	• Books • Photos of personal travels • Diplomas/Certification wall hangings • Photos of mentors/teachers • Items that represent precision • Items that represent educated decisions (awards...)	• I am growing and learning new things every day • I am expanding and nourishing my mind every minute of my existence	• Blues increase understanding • Purples access creativity and intuition • Whites for receiving new information.
Physical	• Quality food • Good posture/stacked or straight spine • Eyes Clear • Skin Moist • Finger nails and toe nails neatly manicured and clean • Hair neat and clean	• I am physically fit • I am healthy in all ways	• Reds to stimulate activity, increase activity

Symbols, Key Words, Affirmations and Color to reinforce your goals (continued)

	SYMBOLS	KEY WORDS/AFFIRMATIONS	COLOR BALANCING
Social	• Photos of fun experiences • Mementos from positive social gatherings (dispose of dried items/flowers no later than one year)	• I am supported by friends • I am a reliable volunteer • I am loved	• Oranges for joy and comfort • Yellow for happiness, to uplift and positive communication
Spiritual	• Soul soothing artwork • Relaxing Music • Creative outlet symbols • Fun music • Symbols of positive inner work	• I am balanced • I surround myself with what makes me whole and happy • I am enjoying myself	• Greens for healing and connection with nature • Turquoises for calming and soothing • Browns for stability, nuturing and security

Soul Mapping with F.I.P.S.S. Balance—Aromatherapy to Reinforce Your Goals

Financial	• Cedarwood to decrease stress • Sandalwood to decrease stress, centering
Intellectual	• Basil for clarity when studying • Lavender for relaxation and clarity when being tested and absorbing information
Physical	• Eucalyptus to invigorate • Citrus Aromas… Lemon, Lime or Orange to uplift and refresh
Social	• Camomile to sooth and decrease relationship tension • Patchouli or Ylang Ylang for sensuality and romance • Rose for romance
Spiritual	• Fir Needle for centering and harmony • Frankincense for serenity and clarity during reflection or meditation • Lavender to calm • Sage for purification

Depending on your life experiences, personality, profession, education, social, and spiritual goals, these aromas may be mixed and matched and are not the only aromas that fit in the above F.I.P.S.S. balance process.

Does it Ever Make Complete Sense?

"It takes a long time to understand nothing."

—Edward Dahlberg, *"On Wisdom and Folly, Reasons of the Heart"* (1965)

I HAVE OBSERVED THAT complete life messages rarely fit together at the same time. Our lives aren't neat little puzzles that eventually create a complete picture because the picture changes too often (even from moment to moment). However, there are ways to minimize the chaos so that you're less likely to miss certain messages to expand your awareness and encourage a more gentle learning curve.

I received an email from someone I had done soul mapping work with and she gave me permission to share her story. She was going through major changes and the following email takes you through a roller coaster of emotions as she experienced many changes at an accelerated rate. She recently quit her mainstream job and decided to pursue her "spiritual" ambitions full-time. She was really getting her butt kicked in many areas of life. Adding to the confusion, she couldn't seem to slow herself down to tackle any one area of life.

"... I have been beating myself up again... and while I can get so frustrated (like I am now)... The numerology report (and soul mapping) you originally did for me... was most helpful as it has aptly served as a road map, an adviser, a perspective-builder, and most importantly for me at this time, an inspiration to help me through difficult times and struggles (like now). I (reviewed) my "Life Path" this morning, as I wanted the inspiration... seeking the message, that will continue to keep me on the path that, to me, seems so powerful, yet can also seem so overwhelming. I then went to my personal year (as well as other analysis done on compatibility, business name analysis, etc.)... knowing this could be beneficial to my (romantic) relationship (as well)... he (her romantic interest) has been a teacher in my struggle with my karmic lesson in my fear of 'total commitment' and my inability in the past to show 'true emotion.' I am getting... the lesson in this lifetime...

...This powerful message not only is applying to my most intimate relationship, but it is spreading out in so many other ways, to a much larger audience... The emotional and financial drain that is equally hitting me right between the eyes (author comment: she quit her job in an attempt to aggressively build her new body, mind, spirit business)... despite a fear of sort of free-falling here (I also tapped into my more practical side, to ensure I had a financial buffer of savings to get me through a growth stage) my inner knowing said 'This is it, and the time is now!' Many signs and messages were saying 'Trust the Divine Guidance.' I heard it inside, I was getting messages on the outside... and in rereading pertinent information in my reports from you, I am sure that I am on the brink of something, and just need to hang in there and continue trusting. My personal year... only reaffirms what I am saying and what I am feeling: 'focus on your career... be aggressive in the pursuit of your success'... And it is THIS career... knowing that the work I am now doing is my calling... I realize the impact of a gift I have been given, and charged to do this work, especially for the greater good of others' well-being... Another excerpt for this (personal) year, 'on a spiritual level you will experience a different mode altogether'... Frankly, the most significant realizations for me have occurred over the past few months, the progress I have made in this time period, both personally and professionally can only be stated as remarkable... It's as if I am taking off, yet I can't keep up with it. Wow, that's it!... As I was writing this, it came to me... why all of my friends are concerned about me, particularly those who are also spiritual... that I am not adequately grounded. It's as if I can't keep up with my own thoughts, yet can't seem to stop them... my latest helper is a tape-recorder, so I can record significant thoughts that come to me. (I) started using this more frequently a few days ago.

...I (emotionally) crashed last night... while the information (she taught one of her first classes from her new material) was beneficial, it seemed overwhelming... I started to cry and just couldn't seem to stop (her workshop seemed to overwhelm her students with too much information)... getting such great response from these type of events... but little financial gain... Which leads me to... 'by helping others, we help ourselves,' yet I

can't seem 'to see the forest for the trees' (in my numerology analysis)…
(Signing her name in three different ways)… See, I don't even know
which one I am!!!!!"

The bottom line is she tried to change too many areas of life at one
time. Let's take a top-line FIPSS look:

Financially: She quit her mainstream job that was willing to keep
her part-time. She was developing a new business that may stabilize in a
couple years or more, but the economy was tight. She had money from
savings for less than a year to pay bills as she built her client base.

Intellectually: She developed workshops but the industry was
unfamiliar to her. She was bright and had enough training and drive to
perfect her business over time.

Physically: She actually ended up in the hospital shortly after this
email, due partly to the overwhelming conditions of her life.

Socially: She was developing new "spiritual" friends. She was
becoming more intimate and trusting her romantic interest.

Spiritually: Her inner confidence was shaky. She had major inner
turmoil due to so many changes at one time and expressed it outwardly
as well.

Looking at this from a soul mapping perspective, what would you
choose as the number one priority for her to take immediate action steps
on (Techniquest)? How would you rank them one to five?

All of our problems, challenges, and/or opportunities can't be "fixed"
or "solved" at the same time. It's about choices, Universal timing as much
as your preferred timing, patience and being okay with never having all
the answers. Minimize the chaos connected with life experiences and
you are certain to expand your awareness and create a life of more gentle
learning.

Soul Balanced Happiness

"Total freedom from error is what none of us will allow to our neighbors; however we may be inclined to flirt a little with such spotless perfection ourselves."   —**Charles Caleb, "Lacon" (1825)**

FIRST, THANK YOU. You are the reason I've been given the gift to write. I am certain that there are ten words in *"Soul"utions* that will change your life for the better because it was written for you.

We have the capability of creating a reality that is perfect to our relative standards in every area of life. The key is being conscious when making choices by following our intuition, being aware that everything happens for a reason, having gratitude for what we have, acknowledging that we are all pieces to one big puzzle, and that we are empowered with choices to reach an outcome. It doesn't matter what business or life focus is chosen, these ideas point us in the direction of perfection as we see it from our own eyes. While we can't control our lives, we can help guide it by feeling our way to a soul-balanced happiness.

We will never have all the answers in our financial, intellectual, physical, social and spiritual realities. If we did, what boring lives we'd lead! But striving to handle our lives with grace, integrity and acknowledging the divine order makes it much easier to recognize the gift that it is. Celebrate the divine richness and perfection of your life path everyday!

About the Author

Michelle Payton is an award-winning author and has published *Adventures of a Mainstream Metaphysical Mom* as well as *"Soul"utions.* In addition to her writing, her time is spent celebrating her life, raising three children, and owning and operating an international wholesale company called The Left Side which is known for its quality body, mind, spirit-focused products and services.

Payton's life lessons began in utero, as her mother struggled with the decision of whether or not to continue her relationship with her alcoholic father. A sign of the times, it was easier to stay in a dysfunctional marriage, so the author's childhood revolved around the dysfunctions, dramas and abuse that resulted from addictive behavior. But she grew into a functional adult by following her intuition, being aware that everything happens for a reason, having gratitude for what she has, acknowledging that she is a piece of one big universal puzzle, and realizing her personal power to reach an outcome. She achieved soul-balanced happiness.

Prior to her personal and professional path toward conscious living, Payton earned a Bachelor of Arts degree from the University of Cincinnati, and was an accomplished national brand marketing professional for thirteen years which provided her with extensive advertising, marketing, research, writing and business building background. She, her husband and life partner since 1982, and three children currently reside in Columbus, Ohio.

For more information on The Left Side and Michelle Payton's products, workshops, soul mapping and balancing sessions, visit www. theleftside.com, e-mail: theleftside@aol.com or call 614-785-9821.

Quotations

Index

If you enjoyed this book and would like to pass one on to someone else, please check with your local bookstore, online bookseller, or use this form:

Name _____

Address _____

City _____ State _____ Zip _____

Please send me:

_____ copies of *"Soul"utions* at $14.95 $ _____

_____ copies of *Adventures of a Mainstream Metaphysical Mom* at $13.95 $ _____

Shipping*: $4.00 for the first copy and $2.00 for each additional copy $ _____

Total enclosed $ _____

Send order to:

The Left Side
437 Hopewell Drive
Powell, Ohio 43065

Phone: 614-785-9821
Fax: 614-785-9819
www.theleftside.com

For more than 5 copies, please contact the publisher for multiple copy rates.

*International shipping costs extra. If shipping to a destination outside the United States, please contact the publisher for rates to your location.